CW01431144

HAYAO MIYAZAKI

Animation: Key Films/Filmmakers

Series Editor: Chris Pallant

HAYAO MIYAZAKI

Exploring the Early Work of Japan's Greatest Animator

Raz Greenberg

BLOOMSBURY ACADEMIC
NEW YORK • LONDON • OXFORD • NEW DELHI • SYDNEY

BLOOMSBURY ACADEMIC
Bloomsbury Publishing Inc
1385 Broadway, New York, NY 10018, USA

BLOOMSBURY, BLOOMSBURY ACADEMIC and the Diana logo are trademarks of
Bloomsbury Publishing Plc

First published in the United States of America 2018

For legal purposes the Acknowledgments on p. ix constitute an extension of
this copyright page.

Cover design: Louise Dugdale
Cover image © Yamaguchi Haruyoshi / Getty Images

A catalog record for this book is available from the Library of Congress.

ISBN: HB: 978-1-5013-3594-5
        ePDF: 978-1-5013-3596-9
        eBook: 978-1-5013-3595-2

Series: Animation: Key Films/Filmmakers

Typeset by RefineCatch Limited, Bungay, Suffolk

To find out more about our authors and books visit www.bloomsbury.com
and sign up for our newsletters.

For Nurit, Matan, and Michael

CONTENTS

ACKNOWLEDGMENTS

This book grew out of the many projects that I have been involved with over the last decade, and I would like to thank the many people who supported my work on these projects. First among them are Professor Paul Frosh and Dr. Shunit Porat, who both supported, encouraged, and greatly aided my study and research into Miyazaki's films and Japanese animation. Further thanks also go to Professor Esther Schelly-Newman for her support and to Professor Aner Preminger, whose seminar on intertextuality in the cinema provided me with useful tools and a chance to examine the connection between Miyazaki and the works that inspired him.

Following my study of Miyazaki, I have written about his work for both academic and popular publications. I would like to thank: Tsvika Oren, who edited a special issue on animation for the online journal of the Israeli art school Bezalel, for commissioning and editing an article by me about European motifs in Miyazaki's works; Ben Simon and Randall Cyrenne of the Animated Views website, who ran an article by me celebrating 30 years of Miyazaki's debut feature *The Castle of Cagliostro*; Rami Shalheveth, who published an article by me about Miyazaki's film *Castle in the Sky* in the short-lived Israeli science fiction magazine *Leprechaun*; and Elsie Walker, who published my analysis of *My Neighbor Totoro* and its roots in children's literature in the *Literature Film Quarterly* journal.

Special thanks also go to: Dr. Nissim Otmazgin, for some helpful bibliographical advice provided while working on this book; Jonathan Clements, for reading the book's first draft and providing many helpful comments based on his extensive familiarity with the anime industry and its history (any mistakes are, of course, mine and mine alone), and to Mary Reisel for her help in obtaining bibliographical materials.

Another special thanks goes to the people at Bloomsbury Academic who believed in this book and made it possible: my editor Chris Pallant, Erin Duffy, Susan Krogulski, Katie Gallof, and Merv Honeywood.

Finally, I would like to thank my family—my wife Nurit and my children Matan and Michael, my parents, Yossi and Tzila, and my brother Shai, whose love and support made this book possible.

PREFACE

The initial inspiration for the writing of this book came from a childhood memory—one that I share with many other children of the 1980s in my home country (Israel). Throughout that decade, there was only a single broadcast channel available for us to watch, a public channel whose children's broadcasting hours' content was dictated by an educational agenda. In accordance with this agenda, many of those hours were filled with long-running animated shows that adapted classics of children's literature, among them *The Adventures of Peter Pan* by James Barrie, Louisa May Alcott's *Little Women*, and many others.

One of the earliest of such adaptations to appear on the screen of Israel's public channel, and definitely the most memorable, was *Heart*, based on the 1886 children's novel *Cuore* by Italian author Edmondo De Amicis. De Amicis' book followed the childhood of schoolchildren and the hardships they endure as their country becomes a modern nation-state. The animated show adapted and extended a short story from De Amicis' book, about the courageous boy Marco and his journey from Italy to Argentina to find his missing mother. De Amicis' novel had its share of fans among the previous generation of young Israelis who found the book's patriotic spirit to be a good fit with their own country's national mood in the 1950s and 1960s; by the time the show was broadcasted, many members of this generation had become parents themselves and they enjoyed rediscovering Marco's story alongside their own children, especially as it was given an excellent emotional Hebrew dub and its theme song was performed by one of the country's most beloved singers. And yet, throughout the endless cycle of the show's reruns (almost every summer vacation), there was an element that left both the show's young and old viewers puzzled: why would a show about an Italian boy traveling to South America have Japanese-language credits at the end of each episode?

As subsequent animated shows that adapted classic children's literature appeared on Israeli television screens, featuring a design style that was somewhat similar to that of *Heart*, their viewers became vaguely aware that these shows were produced in Japan; indeed, throughout the

1980s, it was the main exposure (alongside very few science-fiction shows) of my generation to Japanese animation. What we did not realize, at the time, was just how significant these shows were—how, despite adapting western literature, they very much reflected Japanese culture – and, above all, the fact that the production of *Heart* employed the services of a man who at the time was already one of Japan's most acclaimed animators, and who would go on to win an Academy Award in 2003 for his film *Spirited Away*: Hayao Miyazaki.

For me, this realization came toward the end of the previous millennium, when my interest in comics led me to the discovery of manga (Japanese comics) and anime (Japanese animation), further leading me to major in Japanese during my BA studies. It was during that time that I read and fell in love with Miyazaki's manga masterpiece *Nausicaa of the Valley of the Wind*, shortly before being awed by his epic historical fantasy film *Princess Mononoke* (1997). I became a fan of Miyazaki's works and, as I dug deeper into his filmography, I discovered that, along with his longtime partner Isao Takahata, he was indeed one of the people behind *Heart* – or *3,000 Leagues in Search of Mother*, as the show was known in Japan upon its broadcast in 1976. The design similarities between the show and Miyazaki's later acclaimed works were strong, but as I watched and read more of these works, which led me to write my MA thesis about him, I understood that the connection goes deeper into the thematic foundations upon which Miyazaki rose to his prestigious position as Japan's leading animator.

3,000 Leagues in Search of Mother is discussed in the second chapter of this book. Like the other chapters, it examines an important stage in Miyazaki's early career, showing how it inspired his later acclaimed works. Although several books and many articles have been written about Miyazaki in English (an annotated bibliography of recommended sources is included at the end of this book), this book aims to be the first that offers deep examination of his early career in film and television, alongside works of film, television, and literature that inspired him, shaping his style and themes.

But there is more to Miyazaki's early career than mere hints of his future acclaimed works. Anime scholar Helen McCarthy has described her wonderful book *Hayao Miyazaki: Master of Japanese Animation* (published in 1999) as a "Miyazaki 101" introduction to the director and his works. This books aims at being "Miyazaki in context" in its reflection of how Miyazaki grew within the emerging post-World War II Japanese animation industry and how his rise within the same industry is a very important part of his country becoming an animation superpower, a status that it maintains to this very day. The two stories – Miyazaki's rise to prominence and the Japanese animation industry's rise to the same position – are inseparable; each completes the other in showing the richness of styles, narratives, and themes that dominate both Miyazaki's works and the industry as a whole, and this richness strongly echoes throughout the chapters that comprise this book.

The first chapter, "From Fan to Professional," offers a brief examination of Miyazaki's early life before moving on to analyze the many works he was involved with in Tōei, the first animation studio that employed his talents, and the first big animation studio to emerge in post-war Japan. It is no coincidence that Miyazaki found his first job in Tōei and worked on the studio's projects for almost a decade; he fell in love with animation after watching the studio's debut feature-length animated film, *Panda and the Magic Serpent* (1958). This film, other than being an impressive technical achievement, also shows the wide variety of artistic influences that its creative staff drew from many different sources—American, European, and Asian. These sources, alongside mentoring by the studio veterans, provided Miyazaki himself with strong stylistic and thematic inspiration that is evident in his works to this very day, as in his portrayal of strong female characters and a sense of commitment to social justice and solidarity.

The second chapter, "Tall Mountains and Green Gables," examines Miyazaki's role in the abovementioned involvement with animated adaptations of classic children's literature. It is here that Miyazaki, assisted by other former Tōei employees, as well as new colleagues, began practicing a new form of storytelling: unlike the rockling adventure yarns that dominated the Tōei productions, the literary adaptations were a slower affair, following the everyday lives of their young protagonists. More layers were added to Miyazaki's style during the period in which he worked on the project's shows, from his great love for European landscapes, through the familiar character design that is associated with his works, to the many stories he later told of children, their happy childhood, and the eventual need for them to grow up and leave their childhood behind.

The third chapter, "Our Man, Lupin," focuses on Miyazaki's first significant directorial job on the animated series *Lupin the Third*. This series, adapted from a successful manga, represented a first for both Miyazaki, alongside Takahata, and the anime industry as a whole: it was the first Japanese animated television series that attempted to appeal to an adult audience, and it featured elements that were new to both Miyazaki's and Takahata's work up to that point: not only a modern setting filled with vehicles and firearms, but also over the top violence and more than a hint of often humorous sexual innuendo, alongside something of an anti-social atmosphere. All these elements existed in the manga source material upon which the show was based, and Miyazaki and Takahata attempted to take things in their own direction, not always successfully. These early experiments have also led to Miyazaki's further involvement with the titular character of *Lupin the Third* in both his debut feature film directorial job *The Castle of Cagliostro* (1979) and in a new show in the franchise. In both cases, he managed to fit the protagonist within his own creative vision while at the same time remaining loyal to his roots in both the manga and its literary origins in European crime fiction.

The fourth chapter, "To the Valley Below," offers a study of the creation of Miyazaki's biggest non-animated project—the abovementioned epic manga *Nausicaa of the Valley of the Wind*. The chapter explores the many stylistic and literary influences behind the drawing of the series, from classic mythology and Japanese folktales, through works of European comics and animation to American science fiction literature and cinema. The chapter also discusses the feature-length animated adaptation of the manga, directed by Miyazaki in 1984, merely two years after he began drawing the manga and a decade before he concluded it, showing how his perception of the different themes presented in both the manga and the film—environmentalism, war and peace, world politics—have evolved greatly during this period.

The fifth chapter, "Bringing it All Together: Studio Ghibli," explores the beginning of Miyazaki's directorial career in his own studio, showing how the early films he made in this studio are in many ways rooted in the projects he worked on in the two previous decades, projects that have been discussed in the preceding chapters: *Castle in the Sky* (1986) owes much to the adventure films that Miyazaki worked on as an animator during his period in Tōei, but also to the European backdrop of the adaptations of children's literature; *My Neighbor Totoro* (1988) and *Kiki's Delivery Service* (1989) both go deeper in adopting the themes of growing up from good childhood to good adulthood from the literary adaptations that Miyazaki worked on a decade earlier. The chapter demonstrates how Miyazaki's career as a feature-film director was built on the solid foundations of his earlier career as an animator in the early decades of Japan's post-war animation industry.

The sixth and final chapter, "Growing Up in an Uncertain Present," is devoted to Miyazaki's films between the beginning of the 1990s and the conclusion of the first decade of the twenty-first century. As in the earlier Ghibli productions, these films draw influence and elements from projects he was involved with during his early career; but unlike the optimistic atmosphere of the early Ghibli productions, they give these elements bitter twists, inspired by the political and social uncertainty that accompanied Japan as the twentieth century came to a close. Ironically, the films produced during this era have gained unprecedented financial and critical success, even though most of them portray a dark vision of Japan as a country that cannot find a proper path, a vision that is very dominant in both Miyazaki's acclaimed Academy Award winner *Spirited Away* and his final film, *The Wind Rises* (2013).

Many creative elements, as these chapters show, repeated themselves and evolved as Miyazaki's career progressed, but one element is perhaps the most prominent: from the very beginning of his career Miyazaki has brought together narratives and styles from his own country's culture and from foreign cultures; Japanese folk tales and literature inspired him every bit as did foreign children's literature and comics; he was inspired to seek a career in animation after he watched *Panda and the Magic Serpent*, but drew equal inspiration from Soviet, European, and American animated productions; his film *Princess Mononoke*, a great fantasy-historical epic about his country's past, began as an attempt to create a Japanese version of the famous *Beauty and the Beast* legend. The puzzlement that many people in my country's audience felt about *Heart* being a Japanese production telling the story of an Italian boy in South America is actually the greatest strength behind Miyazaki's work: it is undoubtedly very Japanese but at the same time very cosmopolitan. Miyazaki, as I have learned while writing this book, is an expert in recognizing the best storytelling elements from each culture he encounters, bringing these elements together to create a strong cross-cultural appeal. The voyage thorough the different works that shaped this appeal has been a fascinating one, and I hope the readers of this book will enjoy it too.

Chapter 1

FROM FAN TO PROFESSIONAL

In 1958, at the age of 17, Hayao Miyazaki saw the film that changed his life. It was the film that led him to a career in animation, a career that would make him Japan's (and one of the world's) most acclaimed and influential animators, known as the director of such classics as *My Neighbor Totoro* (1988) and the Academy Award winner *Spirited Away* (2001), as well as a source of inspiration for leading animation studios all over the world, such as the American studio Pixar and the British studio Aardman, among many others. The film that set Miyazaki on this path was *Hakujaden* (literally translated as *Legend of the White Serpent* and later distributed in English-speaking territories under the title *Panda and the Magic Serpent*).

Miyazaki was not, by any means, the only spectator on whom *Panda and the Magic Serpent* has left such a deep impression. The film was the first Japanese feature-length animated color film, and its commercial success hinted of Japan's future as an animation superpower. Yet the great influence that the film had on Miyazaki is noteworthy, especially since it was hardly his first exposure to animation or popular illustrations.

Born in 1941 to a well-to-do family that owned an airplane-rudders factory that thrived both during and after the war, Miyazaki had developed his passion for flight and airplanes from an early age, a passion evident in almost all of his films. Another significant childhood experience that influenced Miyazaki was his mother falling ill with spinal tuberculosis, and the threat of orphanhood became an important theme in his later work. Above all, Miyazaki's formative years were marked by the flourishing of Japan's manga (comics) industry, which offered a cheap and accessible form of entertainment for Japan's young readers in the difficult early years of the post-war era.[1]

The artist whose success has become synonymous with the rise of the manga industry is Osamu Tezuka (1928–1989). Tezuka, who had had a passion for comics, animation, and drawing since he was a child, began his professional career as a manga artist after the war ended while studying medicine at Osaka University. Though he completed his studies, it was obvious that he was destined for a manga artist's career: in 1947 his book *Shin Takarajima* (*New Treasure Island*), a graphic novel inspired by western adventure novels and films, sold an unprecedented number of 400,000 copies, and became the first of many classic titles Tezuka would produce in the following four decades.[2] Characters created by Tezuka, such as the boy-robot *Tetsuwan Atom* (known in English-speaking countries as *Astro Boy*) and the brave lion Leo (known in English-speaking countries as *Kimba the White Lion*), remain leading figures in Japanese popular culture to this day, and they were also the first protagonists of Japanese comics to find an audience in the west through the animated adaptations of their adventures.

Tezuka's success inspired many imitators, and his style soon became recognized as the one many people associate with "manga" to this very day: cinematic storytelling, featuring the breaking of single actions into several panels, successive pages that focused on visual storytelling that feature little or no text, and most notably the characters' design—round, "cute" characters with big saucer-eyes. One didn't have to look very far to find Tezuka's sources of inspiration for this design: a fan of the animated films by Walt Disney and his greatest competitors, brothers Max and David Fleischer, Tezuka's models for drawing characters were Mickey Mouse and Betty Boop.[3]

Tezuka was not the first Japanese artist to draw in this style either: during the war, Japanese animators drew in a style that closely mimicked the work of American animation studios—especially Disney's and the Fleischers'—aware of the popularity of this style among the Japanese audience. Japan's most ambitious propaganda epics produced during the war directed by Mitsuyo Seo (1911–2010), *Momotarō no Umiwashi* (released 1943, the official English title of the 2008 release by Zakka films is *Momotarō's Sea Eagle*) and Japan's first feature-length animated film *Momotarō no Umi no Shinpei* (released in 1945, the official English title of the 2017 release by Funimation is *Momotarō: Sacred Sailors*), also show the strong influence of American animated productions. Both films carried a strong nationalistic anti-western sentiment: the titular character, a brave demon-fighting boy from one of Japan's most beloved children's fables, was presented in the film as a sponsor of Japan's colonialism in east-Asia, who both leads Japan's animal army in war against the hated western superpowers and protects the native animal inhabitants of an Asian jungle from the greedy ambitions of the same superpowers, also educating these inhabitants in the ways of Japan's modern achievements. But it was impossible to mistake the inspiration for both films' character designs for anything other than American animation—*Momotarō's Sea Eagle* even featured Bluto from the Fleischer brothers' Popeye cartoons as the useless commander of Pearl Harbor, and the character also had a small cameo in *Momotarō: Sacred Sailors*. Tezuka claimed that watching *Momotarō: Sacred Sailors* was a major source of inspiration for his own work.[4]

Through Tezuka's works, Miyazaki experienced his first anxiety of influence. His first attempts of drawing manga, at the age of 18, were compared by people who saw them to Tezuka's style. Miyazaki, who at first denied any such influence, eventually realized that his early works were indeed inspired by Tezuka, and this realization was somewhat traumatic: he collected all of his initial sketches, and burned them.[5] This incident started a rivalry of sorts between Tezuka and Miyazaki—a one-sided rivalry, for the most part,[6] which focused on Miyazaki's attempts to shake off Tezuka's influence, find other sources of inspiration, and develop his own style.

Miyazaki found an alternative to Tezuka's influence in another manga artist, Tetsuji Fukushima (1914–1992).[7] All but forgotten today, Fukushima was a successful artist in the 1950s, whose flagship series *Sabaku no Maō* (*Devil of the Desert*) was an epic swashbuckling adventure with an *Arabian Nights* flavor set in a modern environment, spreading across no fewer than nine volumes. Like Tezuka, Fukushima found most of his inspiration in American illustrations, but he turned his creative attention to the less cartoony and more serious works on the other side of the Pacific: his realistic style bore more resemblance to Milton Caniff's newspaper adventure strips than it did to Walt Disney's cartoons. The epic scope of the story along with the richly detailed designs of exotic landscapes and especially vehicles (cars, tanks, and airplanes) have been noted by Miyazaki as a long-standing influence on his own work, one that surpassed that of Tezuka.

Miyazaki also had first-hand access to foreign animation and comics—of the American kind that influenced Tezuka and Fukushima, at least. American comics were regularly brought into post-war Japan by American soldiers, and with the re-opening of the Japanese film market to American films, American animation—especially Disney features—literally flooded the theatres. And although by the late 1940s the Fleischer brothers were no longer running their studio (it was taken over by their main financier, Paramount, and produced inferior works under the new name Famous Studios), a new generation of young Japanese was just discovering their work; their 1939 feature-length adaptation of Jonathan Swift's satire *Gulliver's Travels* became the first foreign animated feature screened in Japanese theatres after the war[8] and a large volume of their short films—Betty Boop, Popeye and Superman cartoons—was sold for broadcast on Japanese television in the mid-1950s.[9] The Fleischer brothers have been another strong influence on Miyazaki, and he seems to have aspired to draw influence from the essence and themes of their work, while avoiding superficial design similarities to their films of the kind that typified Tezuka's manga.

Then came *Panda and the Magic Serpent*. Like Tezuka's and Fukushima's work, it did not come out of nowhere; in fact, the film's roots in the history of Japanese animation and Japan's visual tradition go far deeper than the works of both artists. *Panda and the Magic Serpent* was produced by Tōei Animation, a studio established in 1948 under the name Nihon Dōga (Japan Animation) by some of Japan's veteran animators, including Kenzō Masaoka (1898–1988) who pioneered the

Attending a screening of *Hakujaden* (titled *Panda and the Magic Serpent* in English) at the age of 17 left a deep impression on Miyazaki, inspiring him later to seek a career in animation. He was especially impressed with the film's portrayal of a strong woman as the protagonist.

use of synchronized sound in Japanese animated productions in the mid-1930s, and especially Sanae Yamamoto (1898–1981).[10] Yamamoto, who by the late 1940s was Japan's oldest practicing animator, started his career in 1924, directing the first Japanese animated adaptation of a western story, the Aesop fable *Tortoise and the Hare*. From there he moved on to a highly eclectic career that included folktale adaptations, educational films for schools, and wartime propaganda.[11] Yamamoto's works as an animator show a strong influence from traditional Japanese painting and European animation, notably the work of German cutout animation pioneer Lotte Reiniger (1899–1981), renowned for the silhouette-aesthetic of her films. By the time Nihon Dōga was founded, Yamamoto had largely left the creative side of animation production to focus on his administrative duties, but his high-brow artistic approach is definitely felt in the studio's early productions.

As production in Nihon Dōga grew, younger talent was recruited. Two rising stars in the studio, Yasuji Mori and Yasuo Ōtsuka, would become Miyazaki's mentors, and in many respects it can be argued that they have shaped his ideal perception of animation. Mori (1925–1992), a graduate of design studies, was drawn to animation after being impressed with Masaoka's 1943 musical animated short *The Spider and the Tulip*. He began his career at Nihon Dōga while still working as a commercial artist designing stores, trained under Masaoka himself, and held both jobs until the studio was bought by Tōei and could provide him with a steady income—by which point he was considered one of its top animators, in charge of training new recruits.[12] His style, especially when it comes to character design, was a radical departure from the popular round look that dominated the works of Tezuka and his imitators: while keeping the western-looking big eyes, Mori's work features a greater variety of geometrical shapes—not necessarily in accordance with realistic body proportions—when illustrating bodies and heads, with the result reminiscent of the stylized works of the American UPA animation studio or east-European animation. Despite his great influence on the studio productions, most of Mori's animation duties were in the design and animation departments, and he has directed only two short films. *Koneko no Rakugaki* (*The Kitten's Graffiti*) from 1957 is a tale of a little kitten, whose wall-paintings are coming to life. Cleverly playing with tones in its black-and-white palette, and seamlessly combining sketchy and detailed illustrations, drawing compliments for its ability to convey strong emotions on behalf of the characters through animation with no dialogue,[13] this heartwarming 13-minute film also touched upon the conflict between the imaginative playfulness of childhood and the strict discipline of adulthood—a conflict that would also find its way into Miyazaki's works. Mori's second directorial effort, *Koneko no Studio* (*The Kitten's Studio*), released two years later, was a loose sequel to the previous movie, now following the kitten's misadventures in a film studio. Produced in color, this slick film has its share of hilarious slapstick moments, but it lacks the depth of its predecessor.

Ōtsuka (born 1931) was another animator who came to prominence in the studio, and whose influence can be found in Miyazaki's works—in fact, in 2004, Miyazaki's Studio Ghibli produced a 107-minute documentary about Ōtsuka's work, titled *Ōtsuka Yasuo no Ugokasu Yorokobi*. The film opens with a statement by Miyazaki on the deep influence that Ōtsuka had on his work as an animator. Born in 1931, Ōtsuka's childhood was dominated by his love for locomotives and military vehicles and his talent for illustrating them in loving detail. After a short career as an officer with the Japanese drug-enforcement authorities, Ōtsuka joined Nihon Dōga, trained under Mori, and quickly gained a reputation for his ability to animate dynamic scenes that reflect personality through action.

All the studio's talents, old and new, were put to work on a highly ambitious project once Nihon Dōga was bought by the film production company Tōei in 1956 (the studio subsequently changed its name to Tōei Animation)—the production of the first Japanese animated color theatrical feature. Released two years later, *Panda and the Magic Serpent* was the film that made Miyazaki decide that he was destined to become an animator.

The film's plot follows the love story of Xu-Xian, a young scholar, and Bai-Niang, a mysterious beautiful woman. Love blooms between the two, but once it is revealed that Bai-Niang is actually a demon, an aging Buddhist priest named Fa-Hai vows to put an end to the forbidden romance. A series of tragic events follows, ending with both lovers in exile and separated from one another. Xu-Xian's loyal followers—a pair of resourceful pandas—along with Bai-Niang's loyal handmaiden Xiao Qing, take upon themselves the task of bringing the two lovers back together.

Panda and the Magic Serpent is a fascinating mix of different visual and narrative styles. Adapting a classic Chinese legend about the forbidden love of a scholar and a female snake-demon, the film's initial production reflected the studio's new owners' wishes to become "Disney of the East": it follows the basic Disney formula of adapting classic legends into a family-oriented musical, in which brave heroes save delicate princesses, assisted by cute animal sidekicks, all the way to the happy ending. Yet the production took extra care to give the film a distinctive look, one that could not be mistaken for a western production: Xu-Xian and Bai-Niang, with their traditional clothes and gentle facial design feature a strong Asian appearance, as different as one can imagine from either the fashion-magazine look of Disney features' protagonists or the cartoony design common to comic-relief characters in American animation. The fat, menacing character of Fa-Hai also owes its appearance to the representation of religious figures in traditional Asian art rather than to the stereotypical villains of western culture. The surroundings—from a silent temple to a busy port city—are again the hallmarks of Asian architecture and landscapes. *Panda and the Magic Serpent* is not devoid of western influences: The design of Bai-Niang's handmaiden, Xiao Qing, features the western-inspired big eyes that would be more familiar to today's audience of Japanese animation, and a sub-plot in the film about a criminal gang of animals led by a greedy pig bears strong resemblance (in both look and narrative) to characters from the 1954 animated adaptation of George Orwell's *Animal Farm*, directed by veteran British animators John Halas and Joy Batchelor. The seamless weaving of visual and narrative elements from the east and the west can be considered the film's greatest achievement.

An even greater appeal, however, can be found in the film's portrayal of the struggle between society and the individual, and the latter's ultimate victory. Love blooms between the film's leads against all odds and against any acceptable social norm; Fa-Hai attempts to keep the two apart not because of a vicious nature or jealousy—he truly believes that the affair will have personal and social tragic consequences. The rebellion against this world of harsh norms, a world that keeps lovers apart, comes not from the male lead Xu-Xian, but from the female lead Bai-Niang: while Xu-Xian is sent to exile and does nothing but suffer, Bai-Niang confronts Fa-Hai and struggles for her right to be loved and be a part of the human world. She even goes as far as sacrificing her immortal identity, agreeing to live as a mortal woman, for the sake of her love—the film's happy ending comes at a price. The characters of Bai-Niang and her handmaiden Xiao Qing present surprisingly strong and independent female role-models for the film's young audience—sadly missing from the studio's subsequent film productions—and Miyazaki confessed that watching the film made him fall in love with Bai-Niang's animated character.[14]

Panda and the Magic Serpent is a magnificent film, but it failed to make the studio owners' dream of becoming a world leader in the animation industry come true. It did not find markets in Asia, and the limited American release failed to leave an impression of any kind.[15] Still, success within Japan itself was phenomenal, and the studio settled into a routine of producing family-oriented animated features. The studio's early films followed the same formula set by *Panda and the Magic Serpent*—an animated musical, very much in the Disney mold, but with a look and narrative inspired by Asian culture.

Coming to Tōei

In 1960 Tōei adapted the Chinese sixteenth-century literary classic *Journey to the West* into its third animated feature, titled *Saiyūki* (known as *Alakazam the Great* in its North American release). *Journey to the West* tells the story of a Buddhist monk who goes on a quest to bring sacred Sutras from India to China, aided by a company of animals. The mischievous monkey Sun Wukong, known in Japan as Son-Gokū, recruited unwillingly into this company, is the true protagonist of the book, and a cultural hero in both China and Japan. Since the exploits of Son-Gokū have already been adapted into a manga series called *Boku no Son-Gokū* (*I Am Son-Gokū*) drawn by none other than Osamu Tezuka himself, who by now established himself as Japan's leading comics artist, asking for his involvement in the film's production seemed like the natural thing to do.

Watching the film today is an interesting visual experience, as it clearly tries to balance Tezuka's American-influenced design and his sometimes surreal gags (a memorable segment in the film confronts the protagonist with the Greek hero Hercules who guards the Buddhist paradise) with Tōei's more traditional-Asian approach to design and its conservative storytelling. The end result still feels more like a Tōei production, and indeed there are conflicting reports about Tezuka's measure of involvement in the film: Tezuka claimed that his involvement in the production was limited to the studio using his name for publicity purposes, while Tōei animators have testified that—regardless of their reservations about Tezuka's work—his storyboard guided them in animating the film, injecting his style into the production. Either way, the film proved to be a great success.[16]

This success pushed Tezuka deeper into animation production. He collaborated with Tōei on two more films, but after failing to interest the studio in other adaptations of his comics, he opened his own studio, Mushi Production, in 1961. After producing the arthouse shorts *Aru machikado no monogatari* (*Tales of a Street Corner*) and *Osu* (Male) in 1962, Mushi Production set on adapting Tezuka's leading manga titles (mostly those aimed at young readers) into long-running animated television shows, while occasionally experimenting with more adult-oriented arthouse animation. The success of these productions marked the beginning of the end of Tōei's status as a leader in Japan's animation industry: Mushi Production even managed to succeed where Tōei failed, and found an audience for their products outside the country. While adaptations of classic Chinese legends, lavish as they may be, just couldn't hold the western audience's interest, Tezuka's tales (much inspired by American animation) of a boy-robot who fights evil or the adventures of a lion cub proved easier to translate for the same audience.

This success came at a price, however: Mushi Production managed to produce a large amount of content by considerably lowering the quality of animation in both design and frame-rate compared with the standards set by Tōei.[17] Faced with the new competition, Tōei had little choice but to succumb to the new standards, at least partially: a TV production unit was opened in the studio, adopting most of Mushi Production's methods, though retaining something of Tōei's familiar style of design.[18] The studio did keep its prestigious theatrical features department running, and kept releasing family-oriented animated features, but standouts became few and far between. The golden age of Tōei's animated features proved to be far too short. Yasuo Ōtsuka has lamented about the necessities of television animation production and the compromises they dictated in terms of both animation quality and storytelling, but came to the realization that there is no choice on the matter, and that these new standards are signaling the direction for the animation and global industry as a whole.[19]

Such was the atmosphere in the studio when Miyazaki finally realized his dream of becoming an animator, and was hired by Tōei in 1963, shortly after completing his studies in the prestigious Gakushūin University. Miyazaki's academic background hardly seemed like the kind that leads to an animator's career—in the university, he studied politics and economics, rather than art. Yet his love for art and literature did not fade, as evident by his membership of a children's literature research society during his studies, and the radical left-wing worldview he adopted in those years probably made him reject the idea of taking part in Japan's political and economic system. Combined with Miyazaki's love for comics and animation, these factors led him to seek a career as an animator, at the same studio that made *Panda and the Magic Serpent*, the film that made such a big impression on him five years earlier.[20]

Coming to work at Tōei just as the studio was now moving toward lowering the quality of animation to meet the new industry standards, Miyazaki was quick to recognize Tezuka as the responsible party, and his old artistic grudge against Japan's "God of Manga" became even deeper, as he now also saw Tezuka as the man who sank Japanese animation into the world of poor quality and poor budgets.[21] But Miyazaki wasn't letting his new employer off the hook either: soon after arriving in the studio, he found himself serving as the secretary of the studio's labor union alongside fellow animator Isao Takahata.

Six years older than Miyazaki himself, Takahata joined Tōei in 1959, and like Miyazaki he was fascinated with the creative possibilities that animation offered. His partnership with Miyazaki in the studio's union quickly developed into friendship and collaboration between the two animators.[22]

Through Takahata and other animators in the studio, Miyazaki was introduced to and came to absorb new influences from the works of different animators around the world. The most significant influence came from two different adaptations of fables by beloved Danish author Hans Christian Andersen. The first, *La Bergère et le Ramoneur* (literally *The Shepherdess and the Chimney Sweep*, distributed in English-speaking territories under the title *The Adventures of Mr. Wonderbird*) was a collaboration between French animator Paul Grimault (1905–1994) and poet Jacques Prevert (1900–1977). Miyazaki may have been aware of this 1952 animated film even before starting his work at Tōei, as it was released in Japan as early as 1955, but the film's influence on the studio's different animators, as evident in productions discussed in this chapter, has been extraordinarily strong (Ōtsuka was deeply impressed with the film, having seen it shortly before joining Tōei according to the documentary *Ōtsuka Yasuo no Ugokasu Yorokobi*). The film follows two young lovers who—with the help of a witty, resourceful mockingbird—must run away from a pompous, evil King determined to marry the Shepherdess. The film's production proved to be a nightmare for Grimault, and it was initially released against the director's wishes in an unfinished form.[23] But even unfinished, the film's beautiful visuals captured the hearts of many animators worldwide: it tells an exciting, epic adventure story that takes its audience across, above, and below its magnificently painted surroundings, from the heights of a luxuriously decorated king's palace to the underground depths of the common folk, seamlessly combining classic European architecture with mechanical toys, visual (and verbal) delicate poetry with blatant slapstick.

Grimault's film had a huge influence on Miyazaki,[24] which can be seen in many narrative, stylistic, and conceptual elements of his works as an animator and director—from many direct superficial borrowings, to the deeper understanding of an animated world as a multi-layered entity that exists beyond the currently running scene or sequence. An even deeper influence can be found in the film's ideology: Grimault had witnessed the horrors of the Nazi occupation in France, but at the same time also found his great commercial success during the same period (with the German occupation government providing funding and distribution for his films),[25] and this experience strongly influenced the film's political subtext. Underneath all the film's visual gags and delicate romanticism, there is an unmistakable and uncompromising message against fascism and tyranny, about the need to oppose them and about how sometimes the jester that nobody takes seriously is the harshest critic of such regimes—perhaps a somewhat apologetic gesture on Grimault's part, attempting to argue that the cartoons he produced during the occupation period were in a sense a sort of artistic resistance.[26] The film's breathtaking use of heights and depths, which gives it a sense of richness unparalleled in any other animated feature made before it, also function as a political metaphor: the evil king in the film lives in the top floor of the high tower of his palace, ruling over a kingdom of beautifully designed buildings and monuments, though its streets are eerily empty, thinly populated by his servants. Only underneath this kingdom, underground, live the common folk in poverty, without even the privilege of sunlight. As the analysis presented in this book will show, Miyazaki recognized this deeper subtext of the film as well, and its influence also echoes strongly in his works.

The second Andersen adaptation to deeply influence Miyazaki was *Snezhnaya koroleva* (*The Snow Queen*), a Soviet animated production directed by Lev Atamanov (1905–1981), originally released in 1957. It tells the story of Gerda, a brave little girl who goes on a dangerous journey to save her friend Kay from the clutches of the evil Snow Queen who froze his heart and turned him into a mean, but also frightened, boy. Miyazaki saw the film in a screening held for members of the Tōei workers' union, while he still had doubts about his choice of career and the artistic opportunities it offered. Watching *The Snow Queen* renewed his faith in animation and reassured him that there was artistic integrity in his choice of career. Though it doesn't match the depth of *The Adventures of Mr. Wonderbird* (and, for a film produced in the Soviet Union, appears to deliver few ideological sentiments, if any),

The Snow Queen, much like Grimault's film, tells an exciting story of epic proportions that takes its audience in a brisk pace from one exotic Norse-flavored setting to another, each revealing new visual wonders: carefully illustrated Scandinavian city buildings, harsh, unforgiving snowy wastelands, a palace filled with wonders and a dark bandits' hideout.

Another element that made watching *The Snow Queen* such a strong experience for Miyazaki was the film's portrayal of strong female characters.[27] Much like *Panda and the Magic Serpent* before it, and even more so, *The Snow Queen* is a film in which women, young and old, play all vital roles, heroines and villainesses alike. Gerda the protagonist, whose bravery had made a deep impression on Miyazaki, is assisted by other strong-willed women she meets on her journey, such as the princess from the palace who assists Gerda on her quest, the robber-girl who releases Gerda from the captivity of a bandits' gang (a plot that Miyazaki considered every bit as important as the rescue of Gerda's friend Kay), and the wise old women who help Gerda get to the Ice Queen's palace. These characters became sort of archetypes for female characters in Miyazaki's later works. The equally dominant roles given to female characters of less positive stature in the film also influenced Miyazaki: parallels for the heartless Snow Queen (whom Miyazaki viewed as a tragic figure) and the vicious leader of the bandits' gang can also be found in his works. The male characters of the film, on the other hand, seem to take a back seat—perhaps best demonstrated by the passive, helpless role given to Kay.

Early Animation Experiences

After a short training period, Miyazaki began his work as an animator at Tōei. Throughout the 1960s, Miyazaki was often employed as an animator in television shows produced by the studio. Notable shows include *Ōkami Shonen Ken* (*Wolf Boy Ken*), the studio's first television production, which also gave Takahata his first chance to direct. Debuting in 1963, the show followed the adventures of a young boy raised by wolves in one of Asia's jungles, who makes it his mission to protect the jungle and its inhabitants from predators and greedy humans. The show is the first example of an environmentally aware work to involve Miyazaki, drawing its inspiration from Rudyard Kipling's *The Jungle Book* (almost four years before the release of Disney's adaptation of the same book) and Edgar Rice Burroughs' Tarzan books, as well as their popular cinematic and television adaptations. Another inspiration may have been *Momotarō: Sacred Sailors*, which alongside its nationalistic message also presented a joyous vision of harmonious existence in the jungles of Asia, and the "education" of these jungle inhabitants by a human figure who represented Japanese superiority. The Tōei staff members appear to have cleverly borrowed the narrative frame of Seo's film while neutralizing its problematic national and militaristic aspects. *Wolf Boy Ken* provided another archetype that would become a staple of Miyazaki's later works, now for his male characters: the "civilized boy," who comes to the "jungle" of chaos and violence, educates its inhabitants and protects them.

Another notable show on which Miyazaki worked was *Mahōtsukai Sari* (*Sally the Witch*), following a sorcerer-princess from the parallel world of witches who comes to live in the human world under the guise of an ordinary schoolgirl. Adapted from a manga by Mitsuteru Yokoyama (a notable competitor of Tezuka), which was meant to be a Japanese answer to the popular American sitcom *Bewitched*,[28] the show began its broadcast in 1966 and it holds the distinction of being the first show in the popular "Magical Girl" genre of Japanese animation, which focuses on stories about young schoolgirls possessing supernatural powers who often must hide their true identity. Like *Panda and the Magic Serpent* or *The Snow Queen* it was also an animated work experience centered around a female protagonist, and may have further demonstrated to him the appeal of such works.

It was the studio's theatrical features department, however, where Miyazaki managed to make his first big impression. In fact, the first animation project he was ever involved with, as an in-betweener (drawing the movement frames between the first and the last frame in each scene) was *Wan Wan Chūshingura*. Given the official English title *Doggie March* by Tōei but never actually released in English-speaking territories, the 1963 animated feature told the story of a young country guard-dog who vows revenge against a vicious tiger that killed his mother, enlisting the help of a street-wise gang of urban dogs. The film was the third and final collaboration between Tezuka and the studio,[29] borrowing its title from the famous Japanese historical drama *The 47 Ronin* about a gang of Samurai who avenged the death of their master, but having very little to do with it otherwise. Despite a few dark scenes, *Doggie March* is a fun, well-paced adventure, spiced with exciting action and hilarious slapstick scenes, along many impressively animated scenes of running animal hordes (something of a signature for Tezuka, as evident in his early manga work and the animated *Kimba the White Lion*). Very little in the film, however, can be said to have influenced Miyazaki's later work, other than the theme of struggle against tyranny, and the exciting action-packed climax that takes place in an amusement park, recalling the climactic sequences in Miyazaki's later adventure films.

A year later the young animator's work on another feature turned heads in the studio. *Garibā no Uchū Ryokō* (literally *Gulliver's Space Travels*; the film was titled *Gulliver's Travels Beyond the Moon* in its North-American release) was the studio's first feature made with the western audience in mind. Probably inspired by (and perhaps also envious of) the global appeal that Tezuka's productions managed to achieve, the studio embarked on making a film that would capture the western audience by featuring the future dreams of science fiction while relying (thinly) on the plot of Jonathan Swift's novel, already highly familiar to the Japanese audience from Fleischer brothers' animated adaptation discussed above. Alas, it became another failed attempt to bring Tōei's animated products to the western audience.[30] But while the film suffers from problematic storytelling, it is an interesting artistic achievement, especially due to Miyazaki's creative involvement.

Ted, the protagonist of *Gulliver's Travels Beyond the Moon*, is a young homeless boy who finds refuge from the hardships of everyday life in dreams. One night, after watching a film about the exploits of the brave adventurer Gulliver, Ted sneaks into an amusement park, and barely escapes a group of policemen who are not at all happy about his late-night trespassing adventures. His escape brings him to the home of none other than Gulliver himself—now an old man, whose mind is set on making his final voyage, to space. After some convincing, he agrees to take Ted and his companions, a loyal dog and a toy soldier, along with him. Following a lengthy voyage, they find hospitality among a scientifically advanced race that comes under constant attacks by an army of evil robots. Gulliver, along with Ted and his friends, helps in defeating the army of robots and bring peace and safety to their newfound friends.

The most striking thing about *Gulliver's Travels Beyond the Moon* is its look. For a production aimed at getting the attention of the western audience, the film's staff went for a visual approach that can be considered highly experimental: character designs are very stylized, dominated by angular lines, and everyone looks more like living dolls in different shapes and sizes, rather than an attempt to mimic living creatures' anatomy. The film contains many morphing scenes that sometimes wander into the realm of a plain abstract mixture of shapes and colors, as it portrays montages (one memorable montage features the protagonists getting in shape as preparation for their voyage in space) and flashbacks (notably the breathtaking sequence describing the evil robots' takeover of a peaceful planet).

The film's unusual look was softened by more familiar elements—the Fleischer brothers' own *Gulliver's Travels* feature seem to have inspired the look of the aging Gulliver, with more than a hint that the film version of Gulliver's adventure, watched by Ted at the beginning of the story, is in fact the Fleischer brothers' version (the opening scene of the Fleischer brothers' feature somewhat resembles the scene watched by Ted). Another Fleischer brothers' production, the magnificent action-packed *Mechanical Monsters* (1941) episode in a series of animated shorts about the comic book hero Superman, featuring the famous superhero fighting an army of robots controlled by an evil scientist, appears to have inspired the climactic sequence of *Gulliver's Travels Beyond the Moon*, in which the protagonists bravely face off an army of giant robots, armed with water-rifles.

Gulliver's Travels Beyond the Moon opened in theatres when giant robots were already gaining popularity in Japan, largely thanks to Mitsuteru Yokoyama's influential manga *Tetsujin 28-gō*, whose animated adaptation is known in the west as *Gigantor*. The roots of this popularity are evident in the works that inspired the film: other than *Mechanical Monsters*, the design of the robots themselves appears to be inspired by the giant destructive robot that is controlled by the evil king in Grimault's *The Adventures of Mr. Wonderbird*. Another strong inspiration may have been the giant robots from Fukushima's manga *Devil of the Desert*,[31] which Miyazaki had adored as a child. As with *Panda and the Magic Serpent* six years before it, *Gulliver's Travels Beyond the Moon* achieves its visual strengths by seamlessly blending design elements from different sources into a single, beautiful artistic vision.

Unfortunately, from a narrative standpoint, *Gulliver's Travels Beyond the Moon* also marks the point where Tōei's films started falling apart. Though it has many entertaining elements, the film's script just fails in coming together into a strong enough story: it feels like an aimless series of loosely connected scenes, and the exciting parts of the plot arrive too late, after too many introductions and comic-reliefs, funny as they may be. And in a disappointing contrast to their imaginative visual designs, none of the characters are particularly memorable or interesting.

Yet against the film's general narrative weakness, Miyazaki got his first chance to shine. Although, much as in *Doggie Match*, he worked on the film as an in-betweener, the production staff also accepted creative input from the young animator, and his idea for the film's closing sequence—in which the princess of the robots' planet sheds her robotic shell, revealing a beautiful human princess within—gave the film a strong subtext beyond its original script, drawing compliments from both Ōtsuka and Mori, who praised the human touch he added to the scene.[32] In a way, this scene was the reversal of the iconic image from Tezuka's *Astro Boy* (in both the original manga and its anime adaptation, which showed the boy-robot's mechanic interior underneath its seemingly-human shell[33]). Tezuka wanted to show how science and technology can aid humankind while Miyazaki's contribution to *Gulliver's Travels Beyond the Moon* turned the film into a story about the triumph of human spirit over oppression, thinly disguised as a struggle between people and machines. The dawn of a new day over the princess' ruined, yet free planet, ended the film with a strong, hopeful tone—the people can now start over, they can build a better world. The influence of *Wolf Boy Ken* can also be felt here, as Ted is the "civilized" boy who teaches the way of humans to the seemingly-soulless world of robots.

This sentiment gave the film's final scene (animated by Mori), which otherwise would have been very disappointing, a logical context: Ted wakes up, realizes that all the events he went through were merely a dream, and embarks on his own hopeful journey for a better life. Though this point isn't made explicit in the film, Ted's character may symbolize the hopes and dreams of the children who grew up in Japan in the first few years that followed the war, the same generation that Tōei's young animators belonged to: the belief that a better world can be built on the ruins of the old one.

Shortly after working on *Gulliver's Travels Beyond the Moon*, the younger generation of Tōei animators got a chance to prove itself when Takahata finally got to direct his own feature, titled *Taiyō no Ōji Horusu no Daibōken* (literally, *The Adventures of Hols, Prince of the Sun*; the film was broadcasted on television in English speaking countries under the title *The Little Norse Prince*). Takahata saw the film as an opportunity to realize his political ideals, not just on-screen but during production as well: the film was declared a "democratic" production, where all staff members were invited to contribute their ideas. Miyazaki, who worked on the film as a key animator (drawing the key positions for characters in scenes, with the in-betweeners responsible for completing the characters' movements), became the prominent contributor of such ideas, and his credit was finally changed to "scene designer" in order to reflect the major role he played in the production.[34] Indeed, while *The Little Norse Prince* was directed by Takahata, it feels in many ways much more like a template for Miyazaki's later works of epic adventures and voyages through exotic locations. Alas, all the idealism and good intentions involved in the film's production proved insufficient when it came to the bottom line: after an overlong production schedule of three years, the film finally debuted in Japanese theatres in 1968, with the studio (at the time in a very strained relationship with its union activists, chief among them Miyazaki and Takahata) giving it only a limited release with almost no promotion, and it became a box-office disaster.

The film takes place in Scandinavia during an unspecified primitive era. Hols, a young warrior, hears from his dying father about the evil sorcerer Grunwald who slaughtered all the inhabitants in the village his family came from. Accompanied by his bear, Coro, Hols embarks on a voyage to find Grunwald, and becomes the hero of a small village when he kills one of Grunwald's servants that has been terrorizing its habitants. Though initially accepted as a new resident in the village, suspicion soon grows toward Hols thanks to the ploys of Grunwald. The evil sorcerer uses both Drago, a scheming resident of the village, and Hilda, a mysterious beautiful girl that Hols falls for, to make the villagers turn against each other, and in particular against Hols. Hols struggles to win the trust of the villagers, and save Hilda from Grunwald's corrupting influence.

The film's original script, by puppet-theatre playwright Kazuo Fukazawa, took place in Japan and followed a boy protagonist of the Ainu (the native inhabitants of Japan, whose last dwelling place is now the far-north island of Hokkaidō). On the studio's insistence, the film was re-located to Scandinavia, to cash in on the popularity of Norse folk tales.[35] This decision turned out to work to the film's advantage: at its heart, *The Little Norse Prince* is a retelling of Atamanov's *The Snow Queen*, right down to the Nordic setting forced by the studio, though the plot occurs in a much earlier era. The similarities are throughout, notably in the relationship between Hols and Hilda that mirror those of Gerda and Kay: like the "freezing" of Kay's heart, which turned him into a mean, but also frightened and helpless boy, Grunwald's influence on Hilda has turned her into a passive girl, a tool in Grunwald's plots against

Inspired by the Soviet animated feature *The Snow Queen*, Takahata's first feature-length directorial effort *The Little Norse Prince* was actually more significant for Miyazaki, who contributed many ideas that shaped the film's plot; this is where the "civilized boy in the jungle" archetype, common in Miyazaki's later productions, solidified.

the village. Grunwald's end, much like the Snow Queen's, comes from exposure to sunlight—now not only a metaphor for the victory of emotion over heartlessness, as it was in Atamanov's film, but also for the victory of truth over deception.

It is also easy, however, to note some major differences between Takahata's film and *The Snow Queen*, beyond the superficial difference of time and location. The most curious is perhaps the role-reversal between the male and female characters of both films: *The Snow Queen* was a celebration of female empowerment—the story of a strong-willed brave girl, who goes to save a passive and frightened boy from another female character, and gets help along the way from other strong female characters. In *The Little Norse Prince*, it is the boy-protagonist who goes to save a girl from an evil male character. While Hilda isn't as passive as Kay, and in fact shows a will of her own toward the end of the film, throughout the film it is quite obvious that Hols is the active, leading character of the story, whereas Hilda functions as an antagonist, or, at best, as a love interest.

Though Miyazaki was not the only animator working on the film, and this role-reversal cannot be attributed to him alone, it does look odd considering the praise his later works got for featuring strong female characters or the presence of such characters in Atamanov's film, which he adored. One possible explanation can be the action-oriented nature of the film: the film contains several grand action-scenes, such as Hols' fight against the whale and the climactic confrontation between a rock giant and an ice mammoth, and this action-heavy atmosphere may have been seen as unfit for a female protagonist by the film's crew. But regardless of how much input Miyazaki had in shaping the character of Hols, it became a staple for his future male leads. The "civilized" archetype from *Wolf Boy Ken* and *Gulliver's Travels Beyond the Moon* has solidified in *The Little Norse Prince* into what has for the most part remained the typical male protagonist in Miyazaki's works ever since: usually an orphan boy who possesses incredible (almost inhuman) physical strength, and who is also brave, honest, kind (if not always knowledgeable of the acceptable social norms when it comes to manners), pure in heart, and determined to save the people of the "jungle"—either real of metaphorical (in *The Little Norse Prince*, the people of the village who are hostile and suspicious toward both outsiders and each other certainly represent such a "jungle")—from danger and teach them the proper "civilized" behavior. In other words, the Miyazaki male leads tend to be just too perfect, and not all that interesting. They are superheroes with no uniform or alter-ego; their perfect, flawless behavior on the outside is an accurate mirror for their perfect, flawless personality. In this sense, Hols was the first true male lead in a Miyazaki work, even if this work was directed by Takahata.

Hols is also notable for its political message. It is somewhat ironic that while the *Snow Queen*, the Soviet film that inspired it, was made for pure entertainment purposes and showed very little in the way of political subtext, *The Little Norse Prince* was made with a burning political passion. The importance of the community and unity among the people in the face of evil is the driving force behind the film's plot: while Gerda was an individual who took a dangerous journey upon herself, and gained help from other individuals, Hols gains the final victory against Grunwald after uniting the people of the village, and after the failure of Grunwald's attempts to separate them. Strong visual and narrative parallels can be found between *The Little Norse Prince* and the British animated adaptation of Orwell's *Animal Farm* (similar to those found in *Panda and the Magic Serpent*, discussed above)—unity among characters was also presented in Halas and Batchelor's film as the answer to tyranny and fear (the design of Drago's character also recalls the design of the evil farm owner Mr. Jones in *Animal Farm*). Given that the film was made by the studio's union members, this may have been a too-obvious metaphor for their relationship with the studio's management. But it was probably a metaphor for bigger things as well: a call for social solidarity in the economically prosperous Japan of the late 1960s, where big businesses were growing fast and corrupt politics were growing with them.

The Little Norse Prince is certainly a must-see film for anyone who wishes to explore Miyazaki's creative roots, and it features beautiful designs and rich animation. Unfortunately, as a story, it is not particularly well-told. Like many other Tōei films produced since the middle of the 1960s, the film feels episodic and disjointed; there isn't a strong enough narrative backbone to help it rise above a series of loosely connected events. The following Tōei theatrical feature that involved Miyazaki, though far less ambitious in its artistic and political scope, turned out to be a much better film.

Nagagutsu o Haita Neko (*Puss 'n Boots*), directed by Kimio Yabuki, was released in 1969 and became a hit—in fact, the film's success was so big that it led to the production of two sequels (released in 1972 and 1976, respectively), and to the film's cat character, Pero, becoming the studio's mascot to this very day. Miyazaki worked on the film as a key animator, and if *The Little Norse Prince* was his venture into serious, political filmmaking, *Puss 'n Boots* gave him the chance to practice his creativity in an unapologetic pure-entertainment production.

The film's protagonist, Pero, is a mischievous but kind cat, banished from the cat-kingdom due to his refusal to eat mice. He escapes to the human kingdom, where he soon befriends Pierre, a young hapless boy recently disinherited from his late father's fortune by his two scheming older brothers. Through Pero's resourcefulness, Pierre manages to impersonate a noble and win the heart of the kingdom's heiress, Princess Rosa. But things get complicated when Lucifer, an evil ogre-magician, falls for the princess and kidnaps her. With the help of Pero and a band of bandit-mice, Pierre goes on a daring mission to save Rosa from the ogre's castle.

Puss 'n Boots' basic plot came from the classic fairy-tale of the same name by French author Charles Perrault. The production gave Perrault a direct reference within the film by naming the cat protagonist after him ("Pero" is the phonetic pronunciation of "Perrault"), and giving the film a distinctive French feeling in general, mostly when it comes to characters' names such as Pierre and Rosa (the characters were not named in the original fairy-tale). But at its essence, just like *The Little Norse Prince* was an attempt by the Tōei animators to do their own version of *The Snow Queen*, *Puss 'n Boots* was their attempt to do their

Tōei's animated adaptation of the famous tale by Charles Perrault is a fast-moving, action-packed adventure, owing much of its plot to Paul Grimault's *The Adventures of Mr. Wonderbird* and inspiring many of Miyazaki's later action-oriented productions, notably during his involvement in the Lupin III franchise.

own version of *The Adventures of Mr. Wonderbird.* The sharp-tongued animal who brings two lovers together, in a series of adventures that culminates in a disrupted wedding between a beautiful girl and an evil tyrant (who is also a pompous creature, filled with self-importance), followed by a wild chase, is as closely modeled on Grimault's film as it is on Perrault's original tale.

Puss 'n Boots, however, drew inspiration from the more entertaining elements of Grimault's film while avoiding most of its political content. The love story is not between the poor working-class boy and girl as it was in Grimault's film, but between the poor boy and the princess, as in Perrault's original tale and most conservative fairy-tales. The film ends not with the abolishment of monarchy, but with the return of the fairy-tale order, where the princess is back at her throne and her lover (now elevated to true nobility) is set to rule beside her.

The film makes up for its old-fashioned narrative with polished filmmaking. It is a fast-moving, exciting adventure, with many moments of hilarious slapstick and delightful romanticism—one of the film's most charming scenes, in which the loyal cat Pero helps his friend woo the princess by putting words in his mouth, recalls another French hero, Cyrano de Bergerac. The character of Pero steals the show with its witty manners and trickery, but also with its generosity and—as odd as it may be, for an animal character—humanity (at least some of the inspiration for Pero's witty nature must have come from the kitten's character in Yasuji Mori's earlier short films as well, since Mori served as an animation director on *Puss 'n Boots*). But in contrast to Perrault's original tale, the film does not end with the victory of Pero's trickery, but with the revelation of Pierre's true personality, and its acceptance by the princess—eventually, Pero helps his friend by making him realize that he is a great person, regardless of his social status.

The film's climactic sequence, in which Pero and Pierre put an end to Lucifer's plans of marrying the princess, is a masterpiece of action-directing, and its influence can be seen in many of Miyazaki's future works. The breathless chase through Lucifer's castle is not only exciting, but it also gives the audience a chance to examine its architecture and get an idea about its inhabitant: it is a dark, grim, old, and crumbling place, a relic for a culture of the past represented by Lucifer. The character of Lucifer, for all its cartoony design and mannerism that makes it hard to treat it seriously, hopes not only to win the heart of the princess, but to restore its own heritage and lineage by marrying her—a heritage and lineage of evil and tyranny. This is the point where *Puss 'n Boots* comes the closest to following *The Adventures of Mr. Wonderbird*, not just from the narrative angle but also from an ideological one: the climax and the ending of Grimault's film also marked the end of tyranny beyond the happy reunion of both lovers. Of course, *Puss 'n Boots* diluted this ideological message considerably by assuring its audience that once the "bad monarchy" has been removed, the "good monarchy" can come to power. Still, the film should be applauded for its effort to transcend its literary origins.

Another Tōei animated feature that employed Miyazaki's talents, *Sora tobu Yūreisen* (*The Flying Phantom Ship*), was released in 1969. This film was an interesting attempt to give the familiar studio formula of a light adventure-film a stylistic treatment that would bring it closer to the popular Japanese science fiction productions at the time. A string of commercial cinematic and televised hits, from Ishirō Honda's 1954 *Gojira* (known in the west as *Godzilla*) to Tezuka's animated *Astro Boy* inspired legions of imitators and, by the end of the 1960s, Japanese cinema and television were overflowing with giant monsters, giant robots, and brave heroes who fought them. To write the story of *Flying Phantom Ship*, Tōei hired manga artist Shōtarō Ishinomori, famous for creating the influential *Cyborg 009* series in 1964. The series followed a group of teenagers-turned-cyborgs who fight crime and gave Japan its first team of superheroes, the spiritual ancestors of other Japanese superhero teams such as *The Power Rangers.*[36] Animated adaptations produced by Tōei quickly followed, with two theatrical releases in 1967 and 1968 and a weekly television series in 1968. Ishinomori would go on to collaborate with Tōei on another highly influential project in the early 1970s, the live-action television show *Kamen Rider*, which set a template for Japanese live-action shows about costumed-heroes. With his seemingly endless supply of innovative ideas that turned out to be commercial hits, inviting Ishinomori to work on one of the studio's original theatrical animated features must have seemed like a good idea, even though his artistic and educational aspirations were not nearly as high as the animators who worked in the studio.

The film's protagonist, a young boy named Hayato, loses his family in a series of terror attacks launched on his city by the mysterious "Ghost Ship," whose skull-faced captain appears to have a long dispute with billionaire industrialist Kuroshio. Kuroshio is only too happy to adopt the young courageous boy who saved his life during one of the attacks, but as the film progresses Hayato begins to suspect that his new guardian holds dark secrets of his own.

To say that the plot of *The Flying Phantom Ship* is thin would be an understatement. Ishinomori obviously delivered what Tōei management expected him to deliver—something that will hold together a series of action scenes, in the same manner as the now-popular giant monster movies. But the script barely manages even this: the plot's unbelievably stupid twists and turns that reveal dark conspiracies and surprising truths about the protagonist's family have little, if anything, to do with the giant-monster mayhem scenes.

These scenes show some imaginative designs, as do some of the backgrounds (notably Kuroshio's underground laboratory base, which appears to have been strongly inspired by the British puppet show *Thunderbirds*) but their animation and coloring feel lacking, probably due to budgetary limitations. One sequence does stand out somewhat, featuring a vicious attack of a giant robot on a busy urban area, again echoing similar scenes from both the Fleischer brothers' *Mechanical Monsters* and Grimault's *The Adventures of Mr. Wonderbird*, that have already inspired the climactic sequence of *Gulliver's Travels Beyond the Moon*. The sequence in *The Flying Phantom Ship* has a scarier, almost brutal quality to it compared with the previous Tōei feature, as it shows the panic and death caused by the metal monster—and the military forces sent to stop it as well. Miyazaki proposed the sequence for the film,[37] and animated similar scenes in his later works. Another visual curiosity in the film is the design of the protagonist's dog, a Great Dane who reveals his cowardly nature in the face of danger, especially in the haunted mansion where the film's opening sequence takes place. There is more than a passing resemblance between this dog and the titular character of the American cartoon *Scooby Doo*, which debuted several months after the debut of *Flying Phantom Ship*—had someone at the Hanna-Barbera studio seen the film?

Surprisingly enough, underneath all its narrative and visual weaknesses, *The Flying Phantom Ship* does have a deeper message to deliver, and a pretty radical one. The rich industrialist Kuroshio, who is responsible for the high-life style of everyone in the city and keeps all the residents happy with the products of his company (especially soft drinks—one of the film's many unintentionally funny plot points), turns out to be the scheming villain of the story who exploits the people and the government for his own purposes. Underneath the happy consumers' society, a bottomless pit of corruption and suffering is revealed, and the film's director Hiroshi Ikeda intended to deliver a deep sentiment of distrust in Japan's business and political environment.[38]

This anti-establishment and anti-capitalist agenda is somewhat odd when it comes from a film that Tōei has obviously commissioned for pure commercial purposes—as noted above, *The Flying Phantom Ship* is nowhere nearly as artistically ambitious as the studio's other films—but it makes the film no less political than *The Little Norse Prince*, and the way the film reflects its politics actually had significant influence over Miyazaki. *The Flying Phantom Ship* remains a footnote in Miyazaki's early career, but a curious one: its narrative, visuals, and themes have definitely had an influence on him, even though the film itself is an entirely forgettable affair, and the best thing that can be said about it is that running just under an hour, it is thankfully short.

The End of an Era

By the early 1970s the Japanese animation industry was going through significant changes, with television and theatres providing an ever-growing platform for new shows and films, while studios and merchandising manufacturers were only too happy to stand and deliver. The word "Anime" (believed to have first appeared in film magazines in 1962[39]) now became a common term for the country's animated productions, a proud sister for the already thriving manga industry.

Yet the two studios that inspired this boom found themselves struggling at the beginning of the decade. Years of bad management led to Tezuka's resignation from Mushi, and the studio finally closed down in 1973, while Tōei kept cutting down its workforce and budgets.[40] The studio generally shifted its interest from family-oriented productions to science fiction, superheroes, and giant-robot stories that made other studios successful, and while it kept its animated family-features production running (retaining the same design style, which by now seemed rather anachronistic) well into the mid-1980s, it was more a reminder of days long gone.

Miyazaki had already been working on projects for other studios since the late 1960s, which will be discussed in the following chapter, and of the final two films he worked on for Tōei in the early 1970s, one demonstrates the painful decline in the quality of the studio's family features' production line, while the other indicates the great potential it could have realized had more visionary people been allowed the opportunity to give it their personal touch.

Ali Baba's Revenge, as the film was known in its American video release (originally titled *Alibaba to Yonjubiki no Tōzoku*, or *Ali Baba and the 40 Thieves*), debuted in theatres in 1971. It was directed by Hiroshi Shidara, and employed Miyazaki's services as a key animator. The plot takes the now-familiar formula of Tōei's family features—the orphaned boy against the evil tyrant—and transplants it to an Arabian Nights setting. Many decades after the famous legend, the current generation in Ali Baba's lineage includes a greedy and corrupt ruler of an Arabian kingdom, who terrorizes the population using his genie. Huck, a young boy who is a descendent of the leader of the 40 thieves, rises against Ali Baba's reign of terror with his loyal band of cats.

Like *Puss 'n Boots* before it, *Ali Baba's Revenge* is strongly inspired by *The Adventures of Mr. Wonderbird*. The love story is gone, but the other familiar elements are all there: the brave young protagonist, the evil, pompous, and stupid king who uses his secret weapon (the genie parallels the giant robot from Grimault's film), the band of animal familiars that aids the protagonist in his struggle, and the action-packed climax. But while *Puss 'n Boots* was highly successful in interpreting elements from Grimault's film into a fresh and exciting adventure, *Ali Baba's Revenge* is an almost complete failure.

The film makes it clear from a very early point that it's played strictly for laughs, but it's not particularly funny. The various slapstick stunts and visual gags have an unpleasant, over-the-top feeling to them, as if the animators are trying too hard. All the characters have a cartoony design that was meant to contribute to the film's comic atmosphere, but it instead feels sketchy and unappealing, and the film's rather limited use of colors gives the impression of a cheaply made Saturday morning cartoon. As in *The Flying Phantom Ship*, certain visual elements in *Ali Baba's Revenge* stand out: the genie's design has a Dr. Seuss-like charm to it, and an impressive flashback sequence in the film re-tells the original legend of Ali Baba using Lotte Reiniger-like silhouettes. But, like *The Flying Phantom Ship*, the most positive thing that can be said about *Ali Baba's Revenge* is that it's over fast.

Animal Treasure Island (originally titled *Dōbutsu Takarajima*) was also released in 1971, and was the last Tōei project that employed Miyazaki's services (he was one of the film's key animators, and also participated in the development of the script). The film was directed by Hiroshi Ikeda, who also worked alongside Miyazaki on *Doggie March*, *The Flying Phantom Ship*, and episodes of *Wolf Boy Ken* and *Sally the Witch*. It's easily the best film that Miyazaki worked on in the studio, very reflective of the best elements that typified *Puss 'n Boots*, with a strong narrative backbone that most of Tōei's other films lacked. In this version of Robert Louis Stevenson's classic adventure novel, young Jim Hawkins comes into the possession of a map pointing to the location of the legendary pirate Flint's treasure. On his quest to find the treasure, Hawkins gets mixed up with a gang of ruthless pirates, all presented as anthropomorphic animals, led by the evil captain Long John Silver (an anthropomorphic pig). The competition for the treasure becomes even fiercer when Kathy, captain Flint's daughter, enters the picture.

From a creative standpoint, *Animal Treasure Island* is a triumphant return to the studio's early days of films such as *Panda and the Magic Serpent* with its tight, fast-moving plot, which takes both Jim and Cathy on an exciting adventure across the seas, featuring many twists and turns along the way. Of all the Tōei films that Miyazaki worked on, *Animal Treasure Island* features the best script. The film perfectly balances the serious adventure elements of the story with comic relief moments on behalf of the pirates' gang, builds a clever mystery around the treasure's location, which is exposed in an exciting and sophisticated climax, and, above all, after many Tōei films centered around a strong male protagonist accompanied by a weaker female companion, gives the audience an equally strong female protagonist. In many ways, Kathy is a far more interesting character than Jim: her desire to find the treasure goes beyond a desire for riches, and is connected to her own lineage. She is every bit as resourceful and determined as Jim himself, and the friendship that grows between the two characters, after an initial mutual hostility, adds another layer of complexity to the movie.

With *Animal Treasure Island*, Miyazaki closed a cycle of sorts: it is a film that truly captures the magic of the studio's first color feature, *Panda and the Magic Serpent*, the feature that inspired Miyazaki to seek a career as an animator. Like *Panda and the Magic Serpent, Animal Treasure Island* is an exciting adventure of an epic scope, where the female lead makes every bit a difference as the male lead, an element that will find its way into much of Miyazaki's later work. *Animal Treasure Island* was Miyazaki's peak achievement at Tōei, and he left the studio on a high note.

Notes

1 Helen McCarthy, *Hayao Miyazaki, Master of Japanese Animation: Films, Themes, Artistry* (Berkeley: Stone Bridge Press, 1999), 26–27.
2 Frederik L. Schodt, *The Astro Boy Essays: Osamu Tezuka and the Manga/ Anime Revolution* (Berkeley: Stone Bridge Press, 2007), 22–23.
3 Ibid., 43–45.
4 Ibid., 58.
5 Hayao Miyazaki, *Starting Point: 1979–1996* (San Francisco: Viz Media, 2009), 193–194.
6 Tezuka is rumored to have been envious of the critical attention that Miyazaki received later in his career following the success of *Nausicaa of the Valley of the Wind*. See Jonathan Clements, *Anime: A History* (London: BFI, 2013), 131.
7 Miyazaki, *Starting Point*, 194.
8 Clements, *Anime: A History*, 82–84.
9 Jonathan Clements and Helen McCarthy, *The Anime Encyclopedia, 3rd Revised Edition* (Berkeley: Stone Bridge Press, 2015), 836–837 (all references to *The Anime Encyclopedia* are to page numbers in the digital edition).
10 Ibid., 2604–2605.
11 See Clements, *Anime: A History*, 39, Daisuke Miyao, "Before Anime: Animation and the Pure Film Movement in Pre-war Japan," *Japan Forum* 14, 2 (2002): 203–205 and Jasper Sharp, "Pioneers of Japanese Animation at PIFAN," *Midnight Eye* (2004). Available online: http://www.midnighteye.com/features/pioneers-of-japanese-animation-at-pifan-part-1
12 Clements and McCarthy, *The Anime Encyclopedia*, 1704–1705; Seiji Kanō, *Nippon no Animation o Kizuita Hitobito* (Tokyo: Wakakusa Shobo, 2004), 158–163.
13 Kanō, *Nippon no Animation o Kizuita Hitobito*, 164–166.

14 McCarthy, *Hayao Miyazaki, Master of Japanese Animation*, 28–29.
15 Clements, *Anime: A History*, 97–99 and Jerry Beck, *The Animated Movie Guide* (Chicago: A Cappella Books, 2005), 190.
16 Beck, *The Animated Movie Guide*, 10 for Tezuka's input on the issue and Clements, *Anime: A History*, 112–114 for the Tōei animators' version.
17 Schodt, *The Astro Boy Essays*, 63–72.
18 Clements, *Anime: A History*, 125–127.
19 Yasuo Ōtsuka, *Sakuga Asemamire* (Tokyo: Tokuma Shoten, 2001), 112–113.
20 McCarthy, *Hayao Miyazaki, Master of Japanese Animation*, 29–30.
21 Miyazaki, *Starting Point*, 195–196.
22 McCarthy, *Hayao Miyazaki, Master of Japanese Animation*, 30.
23 John Grant, *Masters of Animation* (New York: Watson-Guptill Publications, 2001), 100–101.
24 McCarthy, *Hayao Miyazaki, Master of Japanese Animation*, 53–54; Grimault's influence on Miyazaki will be further explored in the current chapter and throughout this book.
25 Richard Neupert, *French Animation History* (Oxford: John Wiley & Sons, 2011), 100–107.
26 Indeed, several cartoons produced by Grimault during the occupation period as *Lepouvantail* ("The Scarecrow," released 1943) and *Le voleur de paratonnerres* ("The Lightning Conductors' Thief," released 1944) can be interpreted as opposing Nazi ideology of war and tyranny, and even as a call for active struggle against the occupation in France.
27 Hayao Miyazaki, *Turning Point: 1997–2008* (San Francisco: Viz Media, 2014), 410–415.
28 Jonathan Clements, *Schoolgirl Milky Crisis: Adventures in the Anime and Manga Trade* (London: Titan Books, 2010), 324–326.
29 Clements, *Anime: A History*, 126.
30 Beck, *The Animated Movie Guide*, 101.
31 Tetsuji Fukushima, *Sabaku no Mao 2* (Tokyo: Akita Shoten, 2012), 39–42.
32 Ōtsuka, *Sakuga Asemamire*, 116–125.
33 See, for example, Osamu Tezuka, *Astro Boy, Vol. 1.* (Milwaukie: Dark Horse Comics, 2002), 21–22.
34 McCarthy, *Hayao Miyazaki, Master of Japanese Animation*, 31 and "Prince of the Sun: The Great Adventure of Hols," *Nausicaa.net* (2012). Available online: http://www.nausicaa.net/wiki/Prince_of_the_Sun:The_Great_Adventure_of_Hols
35 Noel Vera, "Little Norse Prince (Isao Takahata, 1968)," *A Critic After Dark* (2010). Available online: http://criticafterdark.blogspot.co.il/2010/11/little-norse-prince-isao-takahata–1968.html
36 Fred Patten, *Watching Anime, Reading Manga: 25 Years of Essays and Reviews* (Berkeley: Stone Bridge Press, 2004), 288.
37 "Other Films," *Nausicaa.net*.

38 Hiroshi Ikeda, "The Background of Making of Flying Phantom Ship" in *Japanese Animation: East Asian Perspectives* eds. Masao Yokota and Tze-yue G. Hu (Jackson: University of Mississippi Press, 2014), 287–296.
39 Sheuo-Hui Gan, 2009. "To Be or Not to Be: The Controversy in Japan over the 'Anime' Label." *Animation Studies*, 4. Available online: http://journal.animationstudies.org/sheuo-hui-gan-to-be-or-not-to-be-anime-the-controversy-in-japan-over-the-anime-label/
40 Helen McCarthy, *The Art of Osamu Tezuka, God of Manga* (New York: Abrams Comic Arts, 2009), 186.

Chapter 2

TALL MOUNTAINS AND GREEN GABLES

Miyazaki spent almost a decade at Tōei, working mostly on action-oriented adventure films focused on male protagonists, and these films' sense of quick pacing, alongside grandiose action sequences, certainly influenced his later career as a director. But as the Tōei animation department started falling apart, Miyazaki began working for other studios on productions of a very different nature—slow-paced, focused on the daily life of their (mostly female) protagonists. If the Tōei period of his career taught Miyazaki about animation that's always on the move, his subsequent career in animation taught him how to stand still, appreciating the beauty of the scenery. And while this idea sounds opposed to the idea of animation in theory, it also became a staple of his later work, one to which he owes much of his critical acclaim: the ability to draw the audience's attention to the small, simple details of everyday life and fill them with beauty and magic.

The first such production to involve Miyazaki was *Moomins* (pronounced in Japanese as *Mūmin*), a television series produced by Tokyo Movie (later renamed Tokyo Movie Shinsha), a studio that emerged with the television anime boom of the mid-1960s. Japanese animated adaptations of foreign legends and classic books were not a new phenomenon when the studio began production on the series in 1969; as noted in the previous chapter, Miyazaki himself worked on such adaptations as *Gulliver's Travels Beyond the Moon* and *Puss 'n Boots*. But *Moomins* represented a move to a new territory—the studio had purchased the rights to a successful series of children's books by a foreign author, hoping to score a hit with the local and foreign audience alike.

The book series by Finnish author Tove Jansson (1914–2001) followed the adventures of the Moomins, a family of cute trolls who live in the deep northern forests of Scandinavia. With the first book appearing in 1945, the Moomin series, written and drawn by Jansson in the years following World War II and the great destruction it brought on Europe, was praised for its promotion of peaceful living, and its sensitive, ideal portrayal of family and community life.[1] For the animators at the Japanese studio, many of them Tōei veterans (notably Miyazaki's mentor, Yasuo Ōtsuka), the series' production was an opportunity to break away from action-oriented productions into something new,[2] but the end result was not viewed favorably by Jansson, who did not like the obnoxious behavior of characters in the animated adaptation, and its introduction of violence and modern elements into her stories.[3] Miyazaki was responsible for one such modern element that may have angered Jansson—drawing and animating a military vehicle for an episode of the show.[4] The episode in question may have been the show's twenty-first episode,[5] in which a clunky animated tank makes an appearance in a short sequence. The episode itself is otherwise a non-violent and touching story, concerning a young and seemingly lost boy who finds a home among the Moomins. As it turns out, the child is actually the heir of a royal family who had had enough of the strict life in the palace (his royal life is mocked in a flashback sequence reminiscent of *The Adventures of Mr. Wonderbird* palace sequences) and the episode emphasizes his enthusiasm for the simple, rural surroundings where he finds a new home. But when the boy's royal family arrives and demands his return, he must leave his newfound friends. Although at the episode's conclusion it is made clear that the boy keeps in touch with the Moomins, it is also hinted that the simple, non-royal life that he sought is now forever out of his reach. This episode contains many elements that are featured in the productions that marked a new direction for Miyazaki's career.

East Meets North

Miyazaki left Tōei in 1971. While realizing this meant professional instability, the atmosphere in the studio following its treatment of *The Little Norse Prince* convinced Miyazaki that creative opportunities should be found elsewhere. Having already worked on *Moomins*, he now joined another attempt to adapt a popular work of Scandinavian children's literature, Astrid Lindgren's seminal book series *Pippi Longstocking*. Miyazaki joined Yutaka Fujioka, the president of Tokyo Movie Shinsha, on a visit to Sweden in order to convince Lindgren to sell the studio the rights for her work. This was Miyazaki's first trip outside Japan, and it left a deep impression on him: it was his first exposure to the European landscapes that he knew, up to that point, only from books and films. He remarked that upon visiting the city of Visby he felt as though he stepped into "the world of Grimm and Andersen." The visit further inspired Miyazaki to enrich the sketchbook that he started working on, visualizing what the proposed adaptation should look like, but the effort proved unsuccessful as Lindgren refused to meet the studio's representatives and discuss selling the rights to her work.[6]

Undeterred, Miyazaki began working on a story for an original production that, in many respects, was a retelling of Lindgren's book, with a distinct Japanese touch.

The end result was two short films, directed by Takahata based on Miyazaki's scripts: the 33-minute *Panda kopanda* and the 38-minute *Panda kopanda: amefuri sakasu no maki* (titled *Panda! Go Panda!* and *Panda! Go Panda! Rainy Day Circus* for their release in English-speaking countries), released in 1972 and 1973, respectively, and screened during special children's cinema events held during vacations. Both films follow the (mis)adventures of Mimiko, a 7-year-old orphaned girl raised by her grandmother in a sleepy Japanese town. After her grandmother leaves the town for a trip and Mimiko is left in charge of her house, she quickly befriends a giant panda bear and his cub, much to the annoyance of the authorities of the local zoo from which both bears escaped. In *Rainy Day Circus*, Mimiko and the pandas come to the help of a tiger cub from a traveling circus, again causing much havoc along the way.

The superficial similarities between the two films and Lindgren's books are obvious: Mimiko's look—especially the red hair, tied in pigtails—is strongly inspired by Pippi, and both characters enjoy demonstrating their physical strength (Pippi by lifting heavy animals, Mimiko by standing on her hands). Many of the films' plotlines also mirror those of Lindgren's novel, especially in the portrayal of the embarrassment caused to representatives of the adult society, disturbing the ordered and organized nature of their life and work. Mostly, these are the same representatives found in Lindgren's novel: a local police officer, Mimiko's school teacher, uninvited guests who break into Mimiko's house and the staff of the wandering circus. Other than the plotlines inspired by Lindgren, Miyazaki's choice of panda bears as the protagonist's friends was inspired by the panda craze that Japan experienced in the early 1970s (following China's agreement to deliver two panda bears to Japan's zoos[7]), and perhaps also by the comic relief panda characters in *Panda and the Magic Serpent*.

By re-locating the basic plot of Astrid Lindgren's *Pippi Longstocking* novels to a Japanese environment and an original story, Miyazaki's scripts for the *Panda! Go Panda!* films gave the audience a heroine who longs for a proper family and social life, rather than rebelling against them as in Lindgren's books.

Visually, both films featured the style that later became recognized as being associated with both Miyazaki and Takahata: the loving detail in which the film presents modern society—roads, houses and vehicles—that co-exist with lush natural environment. Traveling outside Japan for the first time in his life had left a significant impression on Miyazaki: on one hand, it provided him with a chance to see the European landscapes that he read of in the childrens' books he studied during his days at the university. On the other hand, upon returning to Japan, he suddenly became aware of how beautiful his home country is—how its natural landscapes are every bit a thing to be proud of as the Europeans are proud of their own natural environment. After working on projects that, for the most part, emphasized foreign and exotic locations, it was Miyazaki's first trip overseas that brought his home-country to the center of his attention and his work. He described the film as an idealized view of Japan that the film's audience should aspire to.[8]

As an unofficial adaptation of Lindgren's beloved heroine, both *Panda! Go Panda!* films are a fascinating case study for a Japanese interpretation of a European children's classic, especially in viewing what Miyazaki chose to keep and what he chose to change.

While Mimiko shares many design and narrative similarities with Lindgren's heroine, the aim of both characters is different. The embarrassment caused by Pippi to representatives of the adult world is intentional: the character makes it her mission to expose the hypocrisy and absurdity of this world and the rules that guide it. Pippi is an eternal child who never grows up, and she represents the idealness of childhood and the joy that accompanies it, as opposed to the grimness in the ordered adult society.[9] Mimiko is different from the protagonist of Lindgren's novel, having absorbed elements of the adult society into her own life. The embarrassment she causes to the representatives of the same society is not the result of her intentional actions, but rather of her friendship with the giant panda bear and his cub. This friendship, in turn, is also an attempt to fit into the same society: adopting the giant panda bear as a "father" and becoming herself a "mother" to his cub expresses Mimiko's longing to belong to a normal, socially accepted family environment, and hints of her wish to grow up—to become a mother herself in the future. A prominent example of Mimiko's attraction to the social world that surrounds her is found in a scene taking place in her school: the mayhem in her class is not caused by Mimiko but by the panda cub, who insisted on following her, and the embarrassment that follows is caused not only to Mimiko's teacher and the school staff, but also to Mimiko herself, who understands (in sharp contrast to Pippi) the importance of school studies. Though both films celebrate the joy of childhood, they also hint that the adult world is something to aspire to.

This seemingly paradoxical approach to childhood—the celebration of it as a period of joyful, reckless behavior alongside the realization that it must, at a certain point, come to an end, and that growing up has its own benefits—became a recurring theme in the following adaptations of children's literature that involved Miyazaki, and it is strongly present in his future works as a feature-film director. The importance of the family structure in the lives of children, and the belief that the family's role is to help children pass from a good childhood to a good adulthood also solidified in the *Panda! Go Panda!* films: like the protagonists of most of the films that Miyazaki worked on at Tōei, Mimiko struggles with the hardships of being an orphan child, but unlike these protagonists this struggle does not take the shape of an epic adventure but rather that of the attempt to find a family. This became another recurring theme in Miyazaki's later works.

These themes found their way to one of the first animated productions directed by Miyazaki. In 1972, he directed a short pilot film for *Yuki no Taiyō* (*Yuki's Sun*), a proposed animated series based on the manga of veteran artist Tetsuya Chiba (born 1939). A pioneering work in the shōujo genre of stories aimed at young girls published in 1963, Chiba's original story went beyond the genre's familiar elements of teen-romance plots and girls with magical powers, focusing on hardships that a young orphaned girl must endure when her adoptive family falls apart, and she discovers the truth about her real parents.

Yuki's Sun was inspired by Chiba's own childhood—the very choice of a girl protagonist was, according to Chiba, inspired by growing up in a family of four brothers, and always secretly wishing that he had a sister. Chiba also had his fair share of childhood hardships: during the war, his family moved from Japan to the occupied Korea and China due to his father's work (and later conscription to the army), and at the end of the war the family had to make a perilous journey back to Japan.[10]

Miyazaki's adaptation of Chiba's manga into a short film, which runs under 5 minutes, aimed at selling a proposed television series, is notable mostly for its portrayal of the titular character—a young, energetic, tomboyish girl, with a kind heart and a strong connection to nature. Major plot points are skimmed through quickly: Yuki's early years in an orphanage, her adoption by a wealthy family in a big city and the friendship that grows between her and the family's sickly daughter, and the financial troubles that Yuki's adoptive family suddenly finds itself in leading to the quest for Yuki's real parents. Even the very short glimpses into these twists and turns of the overall story manage to deliver a lot of emotion, and the background design—especially the pastoral landscapes of the Japanese Island Hokkaidō—are impressively detailed. Touches of the European scenery that Miyazaki saw during his trip to Sweden (especially in the architecture of different buildings) can also be felt. Unfortunately, the pilot did not generate enough interest among producers and broadcasters to be picked up for a series, and fell into relative obscurity before it surfaced again in 2014 as part of a Japanese Blu-Ray release of Miyazaki's works.[11] But much like Miyazaki's work on *Moomins* and the *Panda! Go Panda!* films, it indicated the direction in which Miyazaki's work would go in the following years.

From the Alps to Green Gables

Moomins, which Miyazaki briefly worked on before turning his attention to the *Panda! Go Panda!* films and the *Yuki's Sun* pilot, was part of a children's broadcasting block sponsored by Japanese soft-drinks manufacturer Calpis. Initially titled *Karupisu manga gekijo* (*Calpis Comic Theatre*), the block's programming has changed direction several times, though *Moomins* set the general direction of adapting classic works of children's literature. It was another show, however—*Arupusu no Shōujo Haiji* (*Heidi, Girl of the Alps*) that really set the tone for the shows that followed.[12]

Broadcasted in 1974, the show adapted Johanna Spyri's 1880 novel about a young Swiss girl who goes to live with her grandfather in a mountain village in the Alps, and then must leave the village in order to take a job helping Clara, a disabled girl in the city of Frankfurt. Heidi does not fit well within the urban environment of the city, and becomes sick with longing for her grandfather.

The show was produced by Zuiyo Eizo, a studio founded in 1969, which in 1975, due to financial difficulties, split into the existing holding company and a new animation studio, Nippon Animation, which took over the production of successive *Calpis* shows.[13] The studio recruited many Tōei veterans, chief among them Takahata, whose work on the different shows produced as part of the block gave him extensive directorial experience and deeply influenced the style of his later work. They had equal influence on Miyazaki, who collaborated with Takahata in the production of these shows in different roles. *Heidi, Girl of the Alps* was the first *Calpis* project involving both animators, a collaboration that would make the show and its successors classic works of Japanese animation.

Another staff member who rose to prominence during the production of *Heidi, Girl of the Alps* is Yōichi Kotabe. A former Tōei animator who worked on projects including *Doggie March, Little Norse Prince, Puss 'n Boots*, and *Flying Phantom Ship*, Kotabe revealed his true strength when he joined the original trip to Sweden to attempt to convince Lindgren to sell the rights to her books and later assisted Yasuo Ōtsuka with the character design on both *Panda Kopanda* films, presenting an interesting fusion between the geometrical-angular look that typified the Tōei productions, and the more round look that recalls Tezuka's work. He was put in charge of character design in *Heidi, Girl of the Alps*, and refined his style considerably while working on the show, highlighting characters'

The connection between childhood and nature—later contrasted by the connection between adulthood and urbanism—is a key element in *Heidi, Girl of the Alps*, the anime adaptation of Johanna Spyri's classic children's novel.

eyelids to achieve greater emotional expression, and in essence created the basic design that was later used in Miyazaki's feature-films. For his work on *Heidi, Girl of the Alps*, Kotabe became the first-ever character designer to get an on-screen credit in a Japanese animated production (the position existed before, but *Heidi, Girl of the Alps* was the first to feature an on-screen credit for it).[14]

Miyazaki has described the work on the show as a non-stop effort by the production staff to push the envelope in terms of the quality of television animation productions,[15] and it shows. The first and perhaps most striking thing about the show is its rich background design. Miyazaki was sent to Europe to draw sketches for the show's scenery,[16] and his work resulted in a beautiful, highly detailed look of each episode that emphasizes nuances of time and space. The wild nature of the Swiss Alps is presented in the show in its quiet, pastoral springs and summers as well as violent, stormy winters. The passage of seasons reminds the audience of not only natural cycles but also of the passage of time. In contrast to the colorful nature of the Alps, the city of Frankfurt is presented in the series as an endless, dark labyrinth of urban structures.

It is a monument for the achievement of man, set in stone to last for ages, unaffected by the natural cycles. Other than Spyri's novel, the show's background designs also strongly recall the pastoral beauty of the *Yuki's Sun* pilot film, which also featured a passage from the countryside to the city, and the friendship that grows between an orphaned girl and a sickly girl from a wealthy family.

The show emphasizes everyday life in both environments, and uses them as a metaphor for the conflict between the worlds of childhood and adulthood—not unlike Spyri's original novel.[17] Nature represents childhood, which is celebrated by the freedom of emotion: there is no guiding hand in the beauty of the tall mountains, wild-growing trees, and animals who wander around freely—it is a carefree environment where the individual's desires and emotions can be freely expressed. Much like the young royal heir from the episode of *Moomins* discussed earlier, Heidi becomes immersed almost immediately in this environment: in one of the series' early scenes, in which she joins a herd of goats in one of the fields, imitates their movement, and gradually undresses to her undergarments—out of the dress-codes of the adult world. In later episodes, through her friendship with Peter, a boy her age who works as a goatherd, she gains an even deeper respect towards the "emotional" nature of her surroundings, such as the wild weather, and puts an end to many adult traits of the people around her, such as her grandfather's cold and reclusive attitude, or plans to put down her favorite goat. The childish innocence that guides Heidi's action helps her in achieving these goals, but it is supported by the environment in which she performs these actions: an environment of emotion, where the strict nature of the adult world is not dominant.

The city, on the other hand, represents the adult world. The logic behind the city's architecture (labyrinthine streets and tall buildings that seem to stretch endlessly, as Heidi watches them from the top of a church's bell tower), and the strict attitude of Miss Rottenmeier (Clara's governess) are all representative of social codes and expectations that the individual must meet in the adult world, and that the adult world expects children to adopt from an early age. Miss Rottenmeier is appalled by Heidi's ignorance on a variety of subjects, from table manners to literacy, all adult traits that are not particularly essential in the Alpine village that Heidi came from. Though other members of Clara's family (her father and grandmother) are more sympathetic toward Heidi, and though she learns the skills of the ordered life in the city, it is a painful process that makes her physically ill.

The differences between life in the village and in the city are also evident in Kotabe's character designs for the show: the village characters are mostly typified by the round look, which aims less for a feeling of cuteness and more toward the impression of gentleness. The people from the Alps are deeply connected to their emotional world, and do not leave their childhood behind, as they grow up and even as they grow old. The people from the city are typified by a more angular design that reflects seriousness, adulthood, and restraint (and also a measure of high-class aristocracy, especially evident in the design of Clara's family and household members, as opposed to the hard-working common folk of the village).

Heidi's return to the village not only heals her, but it also heals Clara—after visiting and staying with both Heidi and Peter in the mountains, Clara finally manages to stand and walk, something she could not do in the city. Though this could be seen as a victory of the emotional childhood in the village over the adult life in the city, the show also makes it clear that during her time in the city, Heidi has also absorbed traits of the adult world, and still puts them to use. The most noticeable example is her decision to continue her school studies, a first step toward her own adulthood that will undoubtedly come someday. Though the village environment is presented as a healthier place children can grow in, the show also hints that at some point they will need to "grow out" of what it represents—to accept the adult world while growing up. Again, a good child can become a good adult. As in the *Panda Kopanda* films, *Heidi, Girl of the Alps* did not intend to deliver a simple message about the superiority of childhood over adulthood; rather, it warned against improper adulthood, one that takes the joys of childhood away. In fact, one of the most delightful scenes in the opening credits of *Heidi, Girl of the Alps* features Heidi swinging, carefree, high above the village in the Alps. This scene originated in a sketch drawn by Miyazaki for the unproduced *Pippi Longstocking* project, which presented Lindgren's protagonist swinging above the city she lives in, celebrating childhood joys to their fullest.[18]

But sometimes there is no choice but to give up those joys, as another adaptation that involved Miyazaki demonstrated. Originally broadcasted in 1979 (by which time Calpis withdrew their sponsorship of the broadcasting block, and it was renamed *World Masterpiece Theatre*[19]), *Akage no Anne* was an adaptation of Canadian author Lucy Maud Montgomery's beloved 1908 novel *Anne of Green Gables*. The series followed the story of Anne Shirley, a young girl adopted by aging siblings

Matthew and Marilla Cuthbert, who own a farm on Prince Edward Island. Much like Mimiko and Heidi before her, Anne is also an energetic girl with an active imagination, whose rich inner world and highly emotional behavior often clashes with the strict norms of the society that surrounds her.

Montgomery's novel played an important role in post-war Japan, as it became part of the childhood of many people who grew up during the era. First published in Japanese in 1952, it appealed to many young Japanese readers who, like the novel's protagonist, lost their parents.[20] Anne's complex and sometimes hostile relationship with the adult world that surrounds her can be seen not only as a struggle for individualism, but also as an insistence to have a joyous childhood, despite not having a family in the normative sense.

Again, the first thing that captures the audience's attention on watching the show is the gorgeous design of the scenery. Like *Heidi, Girl of the Alps*, *Anne of Green Gables* is also set in a pastoral area, where the beauty of nature comes together harmoniously with the agricultural achievements of man. And in another parallel with *Heidi, Girl of the*

Many scenes in the animated adaptation of Lucy Maud Montgomery's *Anne of Green Gables* visualize the heroine's romantic fantasies, where her rich imagination idealizes her surroundings.

Alps, it is the hard labor of men and women, under tough conditions that sometimes border on poverty, that makes the connection between the two possible. But the conditions are sometimes so hard that they make man blind to his own achievement—and it is here that Anne, the imaginative protagonist, sees right through.

Though deeply rooted in realistic plotting and design much like *Heidi, Girl of the Alps*, episodes of *Anne of Green Gables* often exposed the audience to the protagonist's stream of consciousness. This begins in the very first episode in which, on her way to her new home, Anne starts giving new romantic names to the locations she sees along the route—a simple pond becomes "The Lake of Shining Water." This idealization of the surroundings testifies not only to Anne's love of nature (which is very similar to Heidi's) but also to her hope of finding a new, ideal social environment that will replace the family she lost. While Matthew is appreciative and impressed with Anne's enthusiasm toward her new home, his more practical sister Marilla is often unable to understand Anne's rich inner world, which is very much reflective of the girl's optimistic young mindset. Throughout the show's first episodes, Marilla becomes determined to educate Anne out of this mindset and lead her on the proper way to adulthood.

Character design on the show was done by Yoshifumi Kondō who was drawn to a career in animation after being impressed by *The Little Norse Prince* and worked as an animator on both *Panda! Go Panda!* films, and later also collaborated with Miyazaki on episodes of *Lupin the Third*, *Sherlock Hound* and *Future Boy Conan* (all discussed in the following chapters). In *Anne of Green Gables*, Kondō had to design the protagonist in several different stages of her life—the show follows Anne as she grows up and matures—and he took extra care not to present her as an outright beautiful character: in the initial episodes, Anne is a small, thin child with only slight hints of the beautiful girl she'll grow into.[21] Despite this complexity, Kondō's designs for *Anne of Green Gables* often feel less nuanced in comparison with Kotabe's work on *Heidi, Girl of the Alps*, as they often fall into the clichéd trappings of the popular shōujo genre. This is especially true of the characters of Anne herself and her good friend Diana; as opposed to the childish innocence applied to young characters by Kotabe, Kondō gave both characters wide-open starry eyes and (in the case of Diana) also elaborately fashionable wardrobes and hairstyles that evoke romantic dreams and the wish to grow up.

This design, however, corresponded with the theme of the passage from childhood to adulthood in the show, handled in a far more complex manner than it was in *Heidi, Girl of the Alps*. In the show Anne is very much aware—and perhaps even secretly envious—of her friend's privileged status: not only does Diana come from a family that is significantly more wealthy than the Cuthbert couple, but she also takes for granted the fact that she grows up in a loving family with a little sister who adores her (which Diana often treats as a nuisance). One of Anne's most significant dramatized fantasies in the early episodes of the show concerns Diana's falling for a man and abandoning their mutual friendship. What may seem to Diana like a natural progression in her normative family scares Anne, who feels she must struggle to have a normal childhood and wishes to prolong this childhood as much as possible. Anne may romanticize her surroundings, but the notion of real romantic love that represents the passage to the adult world scares her.

This is also the source of many conflicts between Marilla and Anne in the early episodes of the show. While skeptical at first that Anne can even be of any help in the farm, Marilla has an even bigger problem with what she perceives as Anne's reckless nature. Anne's overactive imagination and creative nature are in particular a nuisance for Marilla, who sees both as a source of troublemaking and useless fantasies. Yet Marilla is a far more complex adult character compared with the antagonistic Miss Rottenmeier of *Heidi, Girl of the Alps*: she is not merely an adult who cannot understand the world of childhood, but rather a woman who has known many hardships, and has long given up on her dreams, struggling to survive. Marilla often clashes with Anne not only because of what she considers as the girl's bad behavior, but also because she sees in Anne something that she herself has lost, and this loss is still a source for sadness for her.

One such clash between Marilla and Anne demonstrates this loss: early in the show, Marilla suspects that Anne has stolen a brooch that belongs to her, and forces the girl to confess. In an elaborate flashback scene, Anne describes how she played with the brooch and then lost it, leading Marilla to punish Anne severely—only to find out that Anne has made up the entire story, and had nothing to do with the loss of the brooch. The brooch is a very precious object to Marilla: it is a reminder of days long-gone. Upon realizing that she has forced Anne to confess for something she did not do, Marilla feels deep regret: not only did she wrongfully accuse Anne of stealing, but she also tried to rob Anne of her childhood happiness. In confessing, Anne has recruited her imagination—the same imagination she used before for romantic fantasies and the idealization of her surroundings—for a painful experience. It is the first instance in the show when the audience sees how Anne has to let go of her rich, ideal inner world of youth and make a painful transition to the adult world of responsibility and guilt, for the wrong reason.

The same painful passage occurs when Anne—who previously feared the day that her friend Diana will grow distant once she finds her significant other of the opposite sex—is suddenly threatened herself by teasing she receives from a boy. On her first day at school, Anne reacts violently to an insult from fellow classmate Gilbert Blythe, and remains resentful to him in many following episodes. But more than a reaction to being insulted, Anne's attitude toward Blythe is also rooted in the fear of getting close to a boy, a connection that symbolizes the end of childhood. Blythe's own initial insulting attitude toward Anne is rooted in the same fear, yet he is the first to overcome it—as the show progresses, he tries to make amends realizing that he is actually attracted to Anne. For the most part, Anne stubbornly keeps resenting Blythe until the final episodes of the show, when she finally admits she has feelings for him as well—and that she is truly ready to begin her journey from childhood to adulthood. All this, however, happened after Miyazaki's involvement with the show had ended—he left the production to pursue other projects after work was done on episode 15, when Anne and Blythe had just had their first run-ins.

Away from Home

Both *Heidi, Girl of the Alps* and *Anne of Green Gables* have broken significant new ground for the Japanese anime industry. Within the shōujo genre itself, much like Miyazaki's earlier work on *Yuki's Sun*, both shows have widened the spectrum of storytelling and character development from starry-eyed protagonists with either magical powers or romantic dreams (or both) to a more realistic portrayal of girls and both the hardships and beauty of their everyday lives. It was also, as noted at the beginning of the current chapter, a significant departure from the male-oriented adventure stories that both Miyazaki and Takahata had worked on during their time in Tōei. However, between the two shows, the duo also worked on another *Calpis/World Masterpiece Theatre* production centered around a boy protagonist and his adventures, albeit one with an atmosphere that's more oriented toward the project's realism rather than the action fantasies of the Tōei productions. Compared to both *Heidi, Girl of the Alps* and *Anne of Green Gables*, it also gave a more radical interpretation to its literary source material, Edmondo De Amicis' 1886 book *Cuore* (*Heart*).

Italian novelist De Amicis was a former soldier who fought in his country's war of independence, and he published *Heart* after establishing a career of writing about his journeys all over his country and Europe. In *Heart* he turned his attention to young readers, attempting to educate them for patriotism and pride of their state (Italy became a modern, unified and independent state only 15 years prior to the book's publication) through a story that follows a class of young schoolchildren of different social backgrounds.

Despite its simplistic, didactic nature, *Heart* has been the subject of many opposing political interpretations. Though largely seen after World War II as nationalist propaganda of the kind that drove Italy into fascism,[22] the first political figures to adopt the book and its messages came from the left: the vivid descriptions of the hard lives of Italy's lower-class citizens made it popular among members of Italy's Socialist Party (of which De Amicis was a member).[23] *Heart* also found many enthusiastic readers in Japan, which, at the time of the book's publication, had also struggled with the hardships of becoming a modern national state. A testament of this popularity is the choice of Kenji Miyazawa—one of the most important poets of early twentieth-century Japan—to give all the characters of his novel *Night on the Milky Way Railway* (published posthumously in 1934—and also one of Miyazaki's favorite literary works) Italian names inspired by De Amicis' book.[24] By the time Miyazaki and Takahata began working on the *Calpis/World Masterpiece Theatre* adaptation, *Heart* had a loyal following among Japanese readers; several generations of children who read it in their youth became parents who read it to their own children.

Given the popularity of De Amicis' novel in Japan, the great liberties taken by the production staff headed by Takahata seem surprising. The very choice of narrative focus shows these liberties: the series did not adapt the novel's plot, but that of one of the stories read to the novel's protagonists by their teacher. Like other "stories within a story" in the book, the story chosen for adaptation—*From the Apennines to the Andes*—was a short, didactic affair and the production staff had expanded it considerably.[25]

Much like the original story, the show follows Marco, a young Italian boy whose family struggles with the economic hardships the country goes through in the late nineteenth century. Marco's mother, Anna, decides to take a job in Argentina—one of the world's most prosperous economies at the time—to support her husband and children. Shortly afterwards, when letters from his mother no longer arrive, Marco decides to travel to Argentina and find his mother. His journey gave the show its title—*Haha o Tazunete Sanzenri* (*3,000 Leagues in Search of Mother*), broadcasted throughout 1976.

Again, the scenery design prepared by Miyazaki is one of the most impressive elements of the show. Unlike *Heidi, Girl of the Alps*, which took place in two major locations, or *Anne of Green Gables*, which mostly took place in a single geographic location, *3,000 Leagues in Search of Mother* took its protagonist on an epic journey across two continents. The show begins in the Italian port city of Genoa, which—not unlike Frankfurt in *Heidi, Girl of the Alps*—is shown as an endless maze of narrow alleys. But unlike the grim and dark German city, Genoa is also presented as a sunlit, beautiful city where ancient architecture welcomes modern wonders and small pleasures: the citizens gather to watch zeppelins in the sky, attend a show of street puppet-theatre and enjoy the taste of a cool ice-cream in the hot weather. When the plot moves to South America, the scenery becomes more diverse; alongside modern cities there is also the wild, untamed nature, radiant with the same beauty of the kind the audience was accustomed to in other *Calpis/ World Masterpiece Theatre* shows.

Yet against the beauty of the scenery, the show also presents the ugliness of poverty. Poverty existed in the plots of *Heidi, Girl of the Alps* and *Anne of Green Gables*, but in both shows it was more hinted upon and rarely shown. In *3,000 Leagues in Search of Mother*, it is everywhere. It is the driving force behind the plot, forcing Marco's mother to abandon her family. It is ever-present in the hard lives of the people of Genoa, who despite their attempts to lead a happy urban life must struggle to support themselves. It is most vividly portrayed in the scenes taking place in Argentina, the promised land where Marco's mother went to secure a better future for her children; in the show, it is presented as a land of contrasts, where fortunate enough people live in elegant mansions while the less fortunate are forced to eat the remains of food thrown into the trash (as seen in one of the most memorable scenes of the show, in which Marco is horrified to discover how a family that hosts him brings food to its table).

Poverty also turns people against each other. De Amicis' story carried a strong nationalistic message, emphasizing the cruelty of Argentina's local population in its treatment of the young Italian boy as opposed to the kindness of Italian immigrants in the country who are always happy to offer a helping hand. The show did away with the nationalistic themes, showing how poverty can make people hurt even their friends and relatives: there is a truly heartbreaking moment in the show when the audience discovers (shortly before Marco does) the reason that letters by Marco's mother stopped coming—his uncle stole the money she earned and intended to send to her family. Even the friendly Italian manager of a street puppet-theatre, who provides Marco with food and shelter, uses him cynically when he puts on a play based on the boy's search for his mother, a play that ends with an intentionally tragic tear-jerking ending aimed at getting more money from the horrified audience. But Marco is undeterred by such displays of cruelty he encounters throughout his journey; right to the end he keeps believing in human kindness, and on more than one occasion takes a break from his search for his mother in order to help those in need.

Character designs for *3,000 Leagues in Search of Mother* feature Yōichi Kotabe's work at its top form, drawing influence from a wide variety of sources including art books depicting the era and the Italian neo-realist cinema of the 1950s.[26] The protagonist, Marco, recalls the male heroes of Tōei's productions as *Wolf Boy Ken* or *The Little Norse Prince*, yet he is softened by a more round look that emphasizes innocence, and a smaller figure that makes most of the other characters stand tall above him, reminding the audience how young Marco is. Marco's mother is of robust, full figure, reflecting the tough beauty of a woman who is prepared to deal with the hardships of the world for the sake of her family—staying true to the portrayal of women in De Amicis' original novel, which, while mostly featuring female characters in minor roles as traditional mothers, also portrayed them as strong and independent.[27] In his work on the show, Kotabe has largely avoided the shōujo clichés of drawing beautiful characters in favor of designs that reflect the story's realistic nature.

Marco's good deeds eventually go rewarded, as at the end of the show Marco is reunited with his mother who is about to go through a dangerous medical procedure and (as in De Amicis' original story) regains her strength at the sight of her son. Unlike the orphaned protagonists of *Heidi, Girl of the Alps* or *Anne of Green Gables* who struggled to find a new family over the one they lost, Marco struggled against the very possibility of becoming an orphan, and Miyazaki probably felt a far more personal connection to his story—since, as a young boy, he saw his own mother struggle with a lethal disease that threatened her life, yet she managed to overcome it. Unlike Marco,

Miyazaki did not endure a tough long journey of physical hardships as a child, but he must have identified with the emotional hardships that accompanied this journey, the hardships of a young boy who is afraid of losing his mother.

3,000 Leagues in Search of Mother was the most ambitious of all the *Calpis/World Masterpiece Theatre* shows that Miyazaki and Takahata worked on, combining the epic adventure journeys of the kind featured in Tōei productions with the more realistic backdrop seen in other shows produced as part of the project, and featuring a strong social message about the need for solidarity among people. But the show falls short, compared to both *Heidi, Girl of the Alps* and *Anne of Green Gables* when examining its protagonist: unlike Heidi and Anne, Marco does not really develop in the course of the show. He begins it as a clever, courageous, and kind-hearted boy and remains the same all throughout the story. He is again the "civilized" boy who came to educate the people of the "jungle" of cruelty and greed about kindness, and eventually succeeds in doing so. The problem that also plagued the male protagonists of the Tōei productions—being just too perfect—was also present in the show. It would keep appearing in Miyazaki's future works, typified by female protagonists who were usually more interesting than their male counterparts.

Other Journeys

Other than their major involvement with *Heidi, Girl of the Alps*, *Anne of Green Gables*, and *3,000 Leagues in Search of Mother*, Takahata and Miyazaki also had more modest contributions to two other *Calpis/World Masterpiece Theatre* projects—*Furandāsu no Inu* (*Dog of Flanders*) in 1975, based on the novel of the same name by English author Maria Louise Ramé, and *Araiguma Rasukaru* (*Rascal the Raccoon*) in 1977, based on the novel *Rascal, a Memoire of a Better Era* by American author Sterling North. Though Takahata was already a veteran director by the time he helmed both the *Panda Kopanda* films and the different *Calpis/World Masterpiece Theatre* shows, it can be argued that it was these productions that truly allowed him to find his voice; the realistic portrayal of everyday life became a staple for several of his later acclaimed works in theatrical animation.

Miyazaki, on the other hand, despite having significant involvement in both the *Panda! Go Panda!* films and the different *Calpis/World*

Masterpiece Theatre shows, and even making an early directorial effort on *Yuki's Sun*, was still trying to find his own direction. Elements of all these productions would certainly find their way to his later acclaimed works, though through a different approach from Takahata's realism. Throughout the 1970s, he kept refining his directorial skills in other productions, and alongside his work on adaptations of classic children's literature, also got to work on one of the first anime television productions that was aimed at the adult audience.[28]

Notes

1   Layla AbdelRahim, *Children's Literature, Domestication and Social Foundation: Narratives of Civilization and Wilderness* (New York: Routledge, 2015), 34, 175–176.
2   Ōtsuka, *Sakuga Asemamire*, 140–141.
3   Charles Brubaker, "The Animated History of 'Moomin,'" *Cartoon Research* (2014). Available online: http://cartoonresearch.com/index.php/the-troubles-of-moomin/
4   Miyazaki, *Starting Point*, 315. Many thanks to Atsushi Fukumoto for his help in locating the reference.
5   Miyazaki mentions that he worked on "a couple of episodes" in the show; the nausicaa.net website mentions episode 23 (http://www.nausicaa.net/miyazaki/films/filmography.html), while Anime news network mentions episode 24 (http://www.animenewsnetwork.com/encyclopedia/people.php?id=51). Episode 24 is notable for its very *Lupin III*-like caper plot (see the following chapter for details), so it may have been another inspiration for Miyazaki's future productions.
6   Isao Takahata, Hayao Miyazaki, and Yōichi Kotabe, *Maboroshi no Nagagutsu no Pippi* (Tokyo: Iwanami Shobō, 2014), 64–68.
7   Miyazaki, *Starting Point*, 408–409.
8   Ibid. However, Miyazaki also noted that the house that Mimiko lives in is closely modeled on the one he sketched for the unproduced Pippi Longstocking project, which in turn was based on his trip to Sweden. See Takahata, Miyazaki, and Kotabe, *Maboroshi no Nagagutsu no Pippi*, 72.
9   Maria Nikolajeva, "A Misunderstood Tragedy: Astrid Lindgren's 'Pippi Longstocking' Books," in *Beyond Babar: The European Tradition in Children's Literature*, eds. Sandra L. Beckett and Maria Nikolajeva (Maryland: Scarecrow Press, 2006), 49–74.
10 Information taken from Chiba's official site, in English and Japanese at http://chibapro.co.jp/?tbl=work&id=39 and http://chibapro.co.jp/en_index.php?tbl=profile

11　For a discussion of Miyazaki's work on the pilot, see Daniel Thomas, "Hayao Miyazaki 1972 Pilot Film 'Yuki's Sun,'" *Ghibli Blog* (2015). Available online: http://ghiblicon.blogspot.co.il/2015/02/hayao-miyazakis-1972-pilot-film-yukis.html

12　Emily Somers, "An no shinjo [Anne's Feelings]: 'Politeness and Passion as Anime, Paradox in Takahta's Akage no An,'" in *Textual Transformations in Children's Literature: Adaptations, Translations, Reconsiderations* ed. Benjamin Lefebvre (New York: Routledge, 2015), 159.

13　Clements, *Anime: A History*, 149–150.

14　Kanō, *Nippon no Animation o Kizuita Hitobito*, 52–70.

15　Miyazaki, *Starting Point*, 137–138.

16　McCarthy, *Hayao Miyazaki, Master of Japanese Animation*, 39.

17　Jerry Griswold, *Feeling Like a Kid: Childhood and Children's Literature* (Baltimore: The Johns Hopkins University Press, 2006), 10–20, 66.

18　Takahata, Miyazaki, and Kotabe, *Maboroshi no Nagagutsu no Pippi*, 27.

19　Clements, *Anime: A History*, 149–150.

20　Yoshiko Akamatsu, "Japanese Readings of Anne of Green Gables," in *L.M. Montgomery and Canadian Culture* eds. Irene Gammel and Elizabeth Epperly (Toronto: University of Toronto Press, 1999), 201–212.

21　Kanō, *Nippon no Animation o Kizuita Hitobito*, 27–32.

22　Caterina Sinibaldi, "Dangerous Children and Children in Danger: Reading American Comics under the Italian Fascist Regime," in *The Nation in Children's Literature* eds. Christopher Kelen and Bjorn Sundmark (New York: Routledge, 2013), 54–56.

23　David Chapman and Gigliola Gori, "Strong, Athletic and Beautiful: Edmondo De Amicis and the Ideal Italian Woman," *The International Journal of the History of Sport* 27, 11 (2010), 1970–1972.

24　Sarah M. Strong, *Miyazawa Kenji's Night of the Milky Way Railway: A Translation and a Guide* (New York: M.E. Sharpe, 1991), 83–85.

25　Edmondo De Amicis, *Cuore (Heart): An Italian Schoolboy's Journal* (New York: Thomas Y. Crowell Company, 1915), 237–276.

26　Kanō, *Nippon no Animation o Kizuita Hitobito*, 72–74.

27　Chapman and Gori, "Strong, Athletic and Beautiful," 1970–1972.

28　The analysis presented in this chapter on the *Panda! Go Panda!* films, *Heidi, Girl of the Alps* and *Anne of Green Gables* is based and expands upon an article by me published in the *Literature Film Quarterly* journal. See Raz Greenberg, "Giri and Ninjo: The Roots of Hayao Miyazaki's 'My Neighbor Totoro' in Animated Adaptations of Classic Children's Literature," *Literature Film Quarterly* 40, 2 (2012), 96–108.

Chapter 3

OUR MAN, LUPIN

While Miyazaki was making his first steps in the anime industry in the mid-1960s, just as this industry was beginning to grow and find a larger audience in Japan and abroad, the manga industry was already booming and finding its way to new readers. A generation of post-war children who grew up reading comics was now starting its academic studies and entering the job market, and this generation expected comics to grow up as well—which they certainly did. Unlike the self-censorship that the American comics industry accepted upon itself in the 1950s through the Comics Code Authority in response to criticism of its content, Japanese publishers faced few restrictions.[1] While children's manga continued to thrive, adult readers soon found more than enough sophisticated stories of crime, sex, and politics on the shelves.

One such adult title was *Lupin III*, drawn and written by artist Kazuhiko Katō who published his work under the pen-name Monkey Punch. The series followed the exploits of Arsene Lupin the Third, a daring thief and the leader of a criminal gang consisting of gunslinger Daisuke Jigen, swordsman Goemon Ishikawa, and femme fatale Fujiko Mine. The series follows Lupin as he gets mixed up in hair-raising adventures both on solo efforts and with his gang, often outsmarting Inspector Zenigata, a police detective obsessed with his capture.

Katō drew inspiration from a wide variety of sources while drawing the series, mostly American: it had the narrative of Hollywood thrillers, the violent slapstick humor of American cartoons and character designs featuring exaggerated, twisted body proportions and facial expressions reminiscent of the satirical publication *Mad* magazine.[2] The main inspiration for the series, however, came from a foreign classic work of modern crime fiction.

Lupin III, the series' protagonist, is the grandson of Arsene Lupin, the hero of a series of novels written by French novelist Maurice Leblanc

(1864–1941), published throughout the first four decades of the twentieth century. Leblanc's Lupin was a master thief who always managed to outsmart the law and escape with the loot, but also a gentleman who often fought for just causes on the wrong side of the law. The "Gentleman Thief" archetype of contemporary crime fiction, alongside the caper plots of the same genre that follow the perfect crime from planning to execution, owe much of their early development to Leblanc's novels.[3] At the height of his popularity, Leblanc's Lupin was the greatest literary rival of the famous English detective Sherlock Holmes created by Sir Arthur Conan Doyle; Leblanc himself made this rivalry a personal one when he confronted Lupin with Holmes in one of Lupin's early stories; threats of legal action by Doyle made Leblanc change the name to "Herlock Sholmes" in subsequent editions and future novels.[4]

While Katō's Lupin inherited his literary grandfather's talent, he had none of his gentlemanly manner. In fact, in Katō's stories, Lupin III appears to lack any kind of moral sense whatsoever. He would often backstab his own gang members to increase his share of the profit (his gang members would do exactly the same, given the opportunity), violently abuse people for his sadistic amusement, and though the romantic attitude of Leblanc's Lupin will probably seem chauvinistic by today's standards, he would have undoubtedly rolled in his grave if he had witnessed his grandson's behavior toward women—always rude, often crossing the line to pure sexual harassment[5]—and even the comedic nature of series, aimed at satirizing rather than promoting the anti-social behavior portrayed in them couldn't mask the bad taste that they often displayed.

But it was the anti-social attitude that gave Katō's series much of its early appeal, as Miyazaki himself explains in an article he wrote about the character.[6] Katō's Lupin was both a daring hero who fought the corrupt economic system, but also enjoyed the many benefits that this system brought with it: gourmet food, fashionable clothing, and fast cars. These conflicting sentiments found great appeal among the rebellious Japanese youth of the 1960s, whose country was still celebrating its amazing post-war recovery.

The popularity of Lupin III drew the attention of a group of talented animators, among them Yasuo Ōtsuka, Miyazaki's mentor in Tōei. In 1969 the group produced a 13-minute pilot, in an attempt to convince Tokyo Movie (the studio that would later produce the *Panda! Go Panda!* films) to greenlight an animated series. The pilot alternates between short narrated sequences that introduce the different characters and a loose plot in which Lupin and his gang attempt to escape from a house surrounded by police units commanded by Zenigata. All the hallmarks of the manga series were present: hyper-violence, wild slapstick humor, an eager Lupin who tries to make a move on a naked Fujiko (and is painfully punished), carefully drawn vehicles (Ōtsuka's specialty) alongside widely caricaturized and even somewhat sketchy character designs, and a grandiose conclusion that makes Zenigata realize too late that he has been fooled by Lupin. The psychedelic color-display that accompanied the introduction of Fujiko, alongside the mix of several musical styles in the soundtrack throughout the pilot—jazz, soft rock, and elevator music—gave it an attractive 1960s vibe. While by no means a great example of storytelling, the pilot was a fine demonstration of kinetic, atmospheric action just waiting for someone to realize its potential.

Unfortunately, nobody did. While the manga industry was well-oriented toward adult readers at the time the pilot was made, animated content was still viewed as aimed primarily at children.[7] Despite the popularity of the original source material, no broadcaster was willing to take the chance of producing anything along the violent and risqué lines of the pilot. The people who produced it went their separate ways, and it remained on the shelf of Tokyo Movie, waiting for more tolerant times.

To Catch a Thief

Lupin finally got his chance to star in an animated series aired between 1971 and 1972, when Yomiuri Television decided to take a chance and air it. It was one of the first anime shows aimed at an adult audience, initially modeling much of its narrative after the original manga—the loose plots focused on Lupin's schemes and his dysfunctional relationship with the rest of his gang (who, much as in the manga, would backstab each other for profit or fun). Ōtsuka was commissioned to work on the show, again bringing his talent for detailed design of vehicles, weapons, and all things mechanical[8] alongside the twisted caricaturized character designs familiar from the pilot (and Katō's original manga). It was in many ways an extension of what made the pilot appealing, but it soon turned out that the Japanese networks were right in their fears that this appeal wasn't wide enough, as ratings just failed to impress. After nine episodes, it was decided that creative changes were needed, and Miyazaki and Takahata were brought to helm the remaining fourteen episodes, sharing the directorial duties on each episode.

As Miyazaki's first directing job (a year before the *Yuki's Sun* pilot discussed in the previous chapter), these episodes are something of a disappointment when viewed today in comparison with his later works. They are also significantly inferior to Takahata's work in the same decade on the *Panda! Go Panda!* films and the *Calpis/World Masterpiece Theatre* shows.[9] Though plots became tighter, they often also felt rushed, and while the dysfunctional group dynamic between Lupin and his gang was gradually abandoned, it appears that the new creative staff did not really know what to replace it with, and other than Lupin himself the show's other protagonists became rather bland and uninteresting characters. However, each of the episodes co-directed by Miyazaki and Takahata is also a very entertaining affair, and the new direction that the show took under their creative control often hints of elements that would become familiar in Miyazaki's later career.

The first episode directed by the duo, "One Wolf Calls Another,"[10] centers around a struggle between Lupin and Goemon over the possession of ancient scrolls that were once the property of Lupin's father. The episode largely portrays its characters in the same way the show did under its previous creative team: Lupin and Goemon clash with each other, violently (though they become best friends by the end of the episode) and Fujiko is an over-sexualized femme fatale who tries to beat both at their own game. But at the same time, the episode also introduces the new direction brought in by Miyazaki and Takahata: the true struggle, it turns out, is not between Lupin and Goemon but between Lupin and a much worse criminal, and the plot is more of a grand adventure centered around the search for an ancient treasure (with a reference to Lupin's family legacy—from Leblanc's novels rather than Katō's manga) instead of a caper aimed at stealing people's money or property.

These elements came into greater focus in the following episode, "The Gang's-All-Here Playing Cards Strategy," in which Fujiko convinces the Lupin gang to help her steal a historical deck of cards that belonged to Napoleon himself and allegedly brings luck to their owner. Stealing the deck, however, appears to bring the gang nothing but misfortune as its previous owner—a greedy millionaire named Mr. Gold—seems to always know where they are and is determined to get his property back and the gang members punished.

Though the episode opens with the familiar setting of Lupin taking someone else's property (with the "ancient treasure" twist of the previous episode), it soon takes a very different direction, as the gang must face the consequences of the crime it committed. The episode also follows its predecessor in assuring the audience that Lupin's intended victim is a much worse criminal—here, a corrupt businessman whose ties with the political establishment and law-enforcement agencies make him invulnerable. Miyazaki's and Takahata's political views echo strongly here, and the episode delivers a none-too-subtle message about the unhealthy connections between money and politics, and the growing presence (in the 1970s!) of supervision over the actions of private people. The episode ends in an explosive climax, borrowing both narrative and footage from the sequence in the original pilot in which Lupin gets his friends out of trouble, with a bittersweet twist that makes the gang realize at the end that the whole criminal ordeal they went through just wasn't worth the trouble.

This "crime doesn't pay" approach, which went very much against Katō's original *Lupin III* stories but fitted nicely with the mood that Miyazaki and Takahata wanted to give the show, was further emphasized in two more episodes. "Target the Cash Counterfeiter" is an unusually dark story, in which Lupin competes with a violent Ukrainian gangster over the services of a legendary retired counterfeiter, who is not even interested in getting back in business. The episode opens with a tongue-in-cheek pun on human greed and capitalism (the citizens of a big city are shocked to see money falling from the sky and begin fighting each other in an attempt to grab as much as they can; shortly afterwards they discover Lupin's stamp on each bill, revealing to them that it's a fake) before moving into the main location—a remote citadel in Eastern Europe where the famous counterfeiter now spends his retirement and does not wish to be disturbed.

This episode showcases Miyazaki's and Takahata's debt to the animators that inspired them, especially Paul Grimault: the design of the citadel's interior as a giant machine—from the inner mechanics of the clock-tower at the top to the many trapdoors and defense mechanisms everywhere—owes much to the design of the evil king's castle in *The Adventures of Mr. Wonderbird*. A final slapstick fist-fight between Lupin and the Ukrainian gangster (occurring, much as in "The Gang's-All-Here Playing Cards Strategy," after the whole criminal affair becomes completely pointless) recalls the many fights between Popeye and Bluto in the Fleischer brothers' Popeye cartoons.

But before this amusing conclusion, the episode takes a tragic turn when the struggle between Lupin and his foe results in the death of the elderly noblewoman who provided the counterfeiter with shelter. The counterfeiter, in response, decides to bring the entire citadel down in a grand explosion, taking his own life in the process. Even considering the fact that the show was made with an adult audience in mind, this shocking turn of events is a chilling reminder of the consequences that a life of crime can have.

The following episode, "When the Seventh Bridge Falls," is even more radical in its interpretation of Lupin's character and narrative—it is the first episode in which Lupin acts completely in the interest of justice. The plot revolves around a nameless criminal who blows up bridges in a big city and frames Lupin for his actions. When Lupin investigates, he discovers that the scheme is part of a plan to rob an armored truck—and finds out, too late, that he has fallen for the trap that the criminal has set for him: he is forced to carry out the robbery, else the criminal will kill an innocent girl named Lisa.

"When the Seventh Bridge Falls" introduces, seemingly out of nowhere, a completely different protagonist from the Lupin the audience had come to know in previous episodes and in Katō's manga; faced with the same situation, the familiar Lupin would have undoubtedly shrugged and walked away rather than save the life of a girl he had never heard of; but in this episode, he takes the attitude of a romantic gentleman, assuring the girl that he is going to save her (with none of the rude attitude that characterized his behavior around Fujiko, and women in general, so far) and getting himself into a dangerous situation where he is hardly in control. The character of Lisa indeed feels like a foreign element in the episode—not only does her name hint of a foreign background, but her design is closer to the round look of the European characters from the *Calpis/World Masterpiece Theatre* shows than to the caricaturized appearance of all other characters inspired by Katō's manga. The episode spends more time on its conspiracy and caper elements than on character development—interaction between Lupin and the girl he saves is kept to a bare minimum—but the notion of an altruistic, selfless Lupin will be revisited.

The next episode of the series is perhaps the only one that could really be called a standout. "Beware the Time Machine" is undoubtedly the zaniest story helmed by Miyazaki and Takahata in the show (quite an achievement, considering that plots were often as over the top and exaggerated as the show's character design) and the only science fiction story among the other episodes that kept the background (if not the action) realistic and down-to-Earth. The episode confronts Lupin with a time-traveler who discovers that, at some point in the future, the thief's

A very different affair compared with other episodes in the first series of the Lupin III franchise, "Beware the Time Machine" is nonetheless a prominent example of Miyazaki's frequent attempts to examine the title character's actions in a critical manner.

descendants will cause his own lineage much grief. His solution to the problem? Going back in time and getting rid of Lupin's ancestors, making him disappear.

"Beware the Time Machine" opens with a terrific scene in which, true to the direction that Miyazaki and Takahata have dictated so far, Lupin pulls a successful heist only to discover that his loot disappears. He is then introduced to Mamo, the time traveler, who informs him in a classic-villain fashion of his plan to make him disappear in a few days. Lupin goes into a hyperactive frenzy, trying to achieve as much as he can in the time he has left, starting with a marriage proposal to Fujiko.

More a hilarious comedy than an action or a mystery-driven story, the episode also gives a glimpse at an unfamiliar side of Lupin—what if the carefree daring thief, who knows nothing but the good life of living for the moment, suddenly has to grow up? Though much like all other elements in the episode, the almost-wedding between Lupin and Fujiko (who is actually quite enthusiastic at the prospect, after rejecting Lupin's advances in previous episodes) is a farce played for laughs, it also hints of the possibility of his character maturing someday, realizing that there are more things to aspire to other than fulfilling greed and lust fantasies. "Beware the Time Machine" also continued Miyazaki's and Takahata's attempt to refine the Lupin mythology beyond Katō's manga, linking it to Leblanc's literary hero in explaining how the grandson of France's most famous thief found himself operating in Japan.

The following episodes backed off somewhat from the radical interpretation that Miyazaki and Takahata gave the show's protagonist up to this point. "The Emerald's Secret," in which Lupin and Fujiko try to outsmart each other in an attempt to steal a precious gem from a Grace Kelly-style actress on the night of her wedding, is a traditional Lupin caper, while Miyazaki and Takahata's contribution appears to be more in style than narrative: the episode takes place almost entirely in a single location—a luxury yacht—in the tradition of the romantic Hollywood thrillers that had great influence on both directors; fittingly, the design of the surroundings and the characters (including Lupin and Fujiko) has a pseudo-European feel that recalls the later *Calpis/World Masterpiece Theatre* productions, and above all else is a charming scene in which inspector Zenigata demonstrates his non-existent talent for dancing. The episode is a pleasant, but otherwise pretty forgettable affair. Two more episodes, "Operation: Jewelry Snatch" and "Lupin Caught in a Trap" are both generic backstabbing-plots of the kind that was common in Katō's manga, following Fujiko's attempt to get rich at the expanse of Lupin and the rest of the gang. "Lupin Caught in a Trap" is notable, however, for a sequence in which Lupin and Jigen take over the Japanese Ministry of Finance's money-printing operation in order to produce enough money to pay the needed ransom for saving their own lives. The sequence pays homage to both the classic 1964 James Bond film *Goldfinger* in the manner in which Lupin and Jigen take over the facility, and Grimault's *The Adventures of Mr. Wonderbird*, which also involved a disruption of a regime's printing-operation (of a different kind). The sequence has a nice payoff at the episode's conclusion, when Miyazaki and Takahata again make fun of capitalism and greed.

Two other episodes played the traditional Lupin caper from Zenigata's point of view. In "Let's Catch Lupin and Go to Europe," Zenigata—who is portrayed as the sympathetic character in the episode as opposed to Lupin's mischief-causing gang—sets an elaborate trap aimed at catching the thief once and for all. At some point, the episode makes the audience believe that he might actually succeed this time around, and though it is nothing exceptional in terms of concept, it is one of the most polished, well-structured, and entertaining episodes in the series. "Keep an Eye on the Beauty Contest," in which the Lupin gang robs masterpiece paintings from a famous art-thief, is a close second; though it ends with the gang members getting their hands on the loot, it also pits them against a greater evil, as in the earlier episodes directed by Miyazaki and Takahata (even including a small role for the villain of "The Gang's-All-Here Playing Cards Strategy"), and leaves Zenigata with a considerable professional achievement at the end, even though the Lupin gang has again managed to escape. It is another highly entertaining episode, if little else, with hilarious sequences featuring the Lupin gang disguised as a news crew (also a homage to a similar idea from Grimault's film).

The concluding episodes brought the elements that Miyazaki and Takahata introduced to the show to a greater focus, beginning with three episodes that dug into the mythology of Lupin's character. "Which Third Generation Will Win?" confronts Lupin with the third generation of his grandfather's rival—the grandson of detective Ganimard, who in Leblanc's original novels always failed to capture the original Lupin, not unlike the endless headaches that Lupin III gives Zenigata. Ganimard's grandson, a famous detective himself, arrives in Japan to secure a special French exhibition and redeem his family's honor by capturing Lupin, much to the annoyance of Zenigata, who isn't at all happy about facing competition. It is another entertaining episode, which pits Lupin not only against Ganimard and Zenigata but also against a variety of high-tech toys and sophisticated security systems, proving that they are no match for him. The power-struggle between Ganimard and Zenigata, very much reflecting the different methods of crime-solving in Japan and Europe (Zenigata's heads-on approach against Ganimard's "logic"-driven and high-tech assisted schemes) adds another amusing layer to the story.

Fun continued with "Catch the Phony Lupin," which begins with a set of daring robberies performed by a thief who impersonates Lupin. Lupin's investigation into the matter brings him to an island full of thieves who, as it turns out, are in possession of a book of tricks written by none other than Lupin's legendary grandfather. Lupin's attempts to reclaim his family's property get him in trouble with both the island's residents and Zenigata, who conducts his own investigation into the matter. Despite a somewhat slow start, once the action moves onto the island the episode turns into a series of chases, escapes, and double-crosses that keep things moving at an almost breathless pace, again hinting at some of Miyazaki's sources of inspiration (this time around, the Fleischer brothers' 1938 Popeye cartoon *Goonland* seems to have been a strong influence). Much like its predecessor, "Catch the Phony Lupin" also makes an amusing observation about how modern life and technology come together with traditional Japanese life (or how they fail to do so).

It was the following episode, "Rescue the Shrewish Girl," which actually shook the foundations of the original source material that the show was based on. In this episode, Lupin comes to the rescue of a young girl who is the daughter of his father's long-retired partner in crime. The girl has no idea of her father's criminal past, nor does she suspect that her loving "uncle" actually holds her hostage in order to force her father to return to a life of crime. So when the famous thief Lupin III suddenly appears, she's less than enthusiastic—and Lupin, who is aware that the girl's father does not wish for her to know the truth about his past, can't really explain the situation.

Though "When the Seventh Bridge Falls" had previously introduced the notion of a selfless Lupin who acts solely to save others with nothing to gain himself, "Rescue the Shrewish Girl" took this concept further; here, Lupin's rescue of the damsel in distress is his initial intention rather than a byproduct of his criminal activity. And even though the short runtime of the episode didn't allow for a deep digging into his motive other than his wish to help his father's partner, it is hard not to wonder if there is another meaningful layer here: the character of the elderly, helpless, former partner of Lupin's father can be seen as a grim prophecy of what awaits Lupin himself in the future, when he will no longer be the youthful resourceful thief who lives the good life and will become an old man whose life of crime took a toll on him. It gives the episode a more serious tone, compared with the other episodes of the series, but this tone actually grows organically from what we've seen in the series so far; while some of the previous episodes have glorified a life of crime, "Rescue the Shrewish Girl" reminds the audience that this life comes at a price.

On its surface, however, the episode is mainly a non-stop chase affair, skillfully developing the relationship between Lupin and the ungrateful girl he tries to save. It climaxes in an exciting train ride that brings to mind classic westerns and even the climactic sequence of *Doggie March*, the Tōei film that gave Miyazaki his first professional experience as an animator. The rest of the episode, unfortunately, suffers from weak design and animation compared with the rest of the series, preventing it from becoming a true standout.

The show ended with two routine, though highly entertaining, caper episodes. "The First-Move-Wins Computer Operation!" basically replays the plot of "Which Third Generation Will Win?", again pitting Lupin against a foreign (this time American) detective who insists on using foreign methods (computer technology) to catch Lupin, much to the annoyance of Zenigata. The episode did make things a little more complicated when it presented an initially overconfident Lupin who almost falls for the trap that the foreign detective has set; toward the end of the episode, wiser and more careful, he manages to outsmart his foe on the way to save his friends. The show's concluding episode, "The Big Golden Showdown!" brought the struggle between Lupin and Zenigata to new heights as the thief is determined to get his hands on a newly-discovered stash of old coins, and the cop is determined to get his hands on the thief. The episode plays all the elements seen in previous episodes—chases, escapes, and complex heists—to their extreme, leading to an end in which no side wins but everyone seems to have fun, in a very satisfying conclusion to an uneven series run.

Unfortunately, for most of the viewers, it wasn't satisfying enough—throughout its entire run, the show failed to gain significant ratings. Perhaps the sudden change in direction that Miyazaki and Takahata brought to it turned Lupin fans away from the show, which wasn't too successful to begin with, or perhaps the audience just wasn't ready for an adult-oriented animated show. Either way, when the show ended, the prospect of a second season did not seem too promising.

The Thief Strikes Again

But Lupin's character, it turned out, was popular enough for his fans to give the show another chance. Though the animated show was not too successful upon its first airing, reruns have managed to slowly build a solid audience. As their popularity grew, the powers-that-be took notice and in 1977 a new Lupin animated series premiered. The series has managed to overcome many of the problems that the previous animated adaptation faced, finding the right balance between the protagonist's darker roots in Katō's manga and the lighter tone brought to it by Miyazaki and Takahata. The new series was also a rousing success, spreading across no fewer than 155 episodes over 3 years, and this success encouraged the producers to expand to the big screen as well.

In 1978, while the new television series was still running, the first Lupin animated feature made its theatrical debut. Simply titled *Lupin the Third* (English-language releases carried the titles The *Mystery of Mamo* and *The Secret of Mamo*), the film was directed by Sōji Yoshikawa, who worked alongside Miyazaki on the first Lupin television series as both a writer and storyboard artist. Adopting the same over-the-top approach set against a fantastic backdrop that characterized the episode "Beware the Time Machine" from the first series, the film took its protagonists on an epic adventure in both time and space. But everything that worked so well on "Beware the Time Machine" went wrong in the new film: compared with the episode's tight script, *The Mystery of Mamo* is an overlong messed-up affair filled with plot holes, and though the film is full of action and chase sequences, they all feel heavy-handed and unexciting, as though the creative team were trying too hard to impress. Regardless of its quality, however, the film was a box-office hit, and production almost immediately commenced on another Lupin theatrical adventure. Miyazaki was chosen to helm the film, titled *Rupan Sansei: Kariosuturo no Shiro* (*Lupin the Third: the Castle of Cagliostro*) and it was completed in an insane schedule of only four months to meet its release date of December of 1979, a year apart from its predecessor.

The film opens with the now-familiar caper in which Lupin and Jigen rob a casino and outsmart its security personnel as they escape with the loot—only to find that this loot consists entirely of faked bills. Lupin recognizes the forgeries from his early days as a thief, when an unwise attempt at robbing a fortified castle in the small European monarchy of Cagliostro almost led to his death. In an attempt to find out how the forged bills suddenly surfaced, Lupin and Jigen make their way to the castle, where they find out the monarchy's current ruler, the evil Count Cagliostro, intends to marry the heiress Princess Clarice to ensure his regime. Lupin attempts to save the princess from the forced marriage, and soon finds himself in over his head as he discovers a conspiracy that involves an attempt to flood the world with forged money and a mysterious treasure hidden underneath the count's castle.

Many narrative and visual elements from the first Lupin television series found their way into the film: car-chases featuring a Fiat-500 and a Citroen 2CV (both cars have made appearances in the television series as well; they were drawn based on Miyazaki's and Yasuo Ōtsuka's real-life cars, respectively), daring aerial escapes, a plot involving a conspiracy of money counterfeiting, and even a tense clock-tower sequence. But in *The Castle of Cagliostro*, all these elements came together in an

The climactic sequence of *The Castle of Cagliostro*, taking place at the top of a clock-tower, inspired many foreign animators and marked Miyazaki's rise to prominence in the global animation community.

unprecedented elegance—indeed, it is not only Miyazaki's first feature-length film as a director, but it also remains the most tightly plotted film he made in his entire career. The script, which Miyazaki co-wrote with Haruya Yamazaki, remains an excellent example of a perfectly paced yarn featuring unforgettable characters, proving that, despite being more or less bound to a single location, *The Castle of Cagliostro* was every bit an epic adventure as its predecessor *The Mystery of Mamo*.

But there is much more to *The Castle of Cagliostro* than a mere adventure. While the first television series sometimes appeared to zigzag between two Lupins—the mischievous daring thief from Katō's original manga and the more altruistic gentleman thief that Miyazaki and Takahata tried to turn him into, *The Castle of Cagliostro* gave the audience a Lupin who is almost completely the latter, and yet it acknowledged the more sinister roots of the character from the manga. True, Lupin's coming to the rescue of the global economy in the film feels out of character compared with the original manga (in fact, the character never went this far in the first television series either), and the delicate romanticism with which he courts the princess is nothing like his rude behavior towards women that the readers of the original manga were used to, but the film hints that this change in Lupin's character did not come out of nowhere—it is the result of many years of living the life of crime, and the toll that these years have taken. The film contrasts the younger, daring Lupin who set upon robbing the castle for his personal gain (in a flashback scene which contains a fitting visual reference to the original Lupin pilot produced a decade earlier) and the older, wiser Lupin who must do it again, this time in the name of a more noble cause.

Scholar Helen McCarthy has pointed to classic Hollywood thrillers as possible sources of inspiration for *The Castle of Cagliostro*, notably Alfred Hitchcock's *To Catch a Thief* (1955), which also featured a protagonist who was a daring thief in his youth and now must put his talents to use in the service of justice.[11] The main inspiration for the film's portrayal of Lupin, however, appears to have been Leblanc's original Lupin novels—especially the twelfth novel in the original Lupin series, *The Countess of Cagliostro* (translated into English under the title *The Memoirs of Arsene Lupin*[12] in North America, and *The Candlestick With Seven Branches* in the United Kingdom).

The Countess of Cagliostro was written when Lupin was already an established character and was presented as a prequel to previously published Lupin stories, featuring a young Lupin who is determined to marry his lover Clarice, over her father's objection to her marrying a commoner. Trying to prove himself worthy to Clarice's father, Lupin finds himself mixed up in an affair involving Josephine Balsamo, a beautiful woman suspected of being the daughter of the notorious eighteenth-century conman Alessandro Cagliostro. Josephine herself is part of a bigger plot to find an ancient treasure related to Clarice's family heritage.

The superficial similarities between the novel's plot and *The Castle of Cagliostro* are obvious—from the choice of names to the plot revolving around an old family heirloom of a young innocent girl named Clarice (this element in the film also appears to refer to the character of Kathy in the Tōei film *Animal Treasure Island*), but the connections between the two works go deeper. The film's Clarice has something of both the novel's Clarice and Josephine: as in Leblanc's novel, she is a gentle, helpless girl, trapped in the traditions of her high-class family. But as the film progresses, much inspired by Lupin, she gains the determination and inner strength of the novel's Josephine, without acquiring any of the latter's negative characteristics of greed and jealousy. Josephine's darker personality traits seem to have found their way to Fujiko's character in the film, and yet compared with her behavior in previous incarnations of the Lupin franchise, her character's portrayal in *The Castle of Cagliostro* is rather tame. She is also after the treasure, and she causes a lot of mayhem, but unlike Leblanc's Josephine, she does not try to come between Lupin and Clarice—perhaps recognizing a lost battle when she sees it.

The Castle of Cagliostro celebrates Miyazaki's love for Europe. The film's character designs abandon the *Mad* magazine-style sketchy look of the first series and the original manga in favor of a more streamlined look reminiscent of both the "clear line" style of Franco-Belgian comics and the *Calpis/World Masterpiece Theatre* productions. These productions appear to have inspired the look of the film's pseudo-European landscapes that combine the beauty of nature with ancient urban architecture. Though the film's fictional state of Cagliostro appears to be modeled on small European monarchies such as Luxemburg, Monaco, and Lichtenstein, Miyazaki claimed that the main inspiration for its look came from Italy.[13]

The main European inspiration for the film, however, came from *The Adventures of Mr. Wonderbird*. Having worked on *Puss 'n Boots*, Tōei's homage to Grimault's film, and having paid his own homage to the same film in "Target the Cash Counterfeiter" and "Lupin Caught in a Trap," in *The Castle of Cagliostro* Miyazaki once more demonstrates the deep influence that the French director had on him. Again, the superficial similarities between the two films are easy to spot in both narrative and visuals, including the basic plotline of disrupting the wedding of an evil tyrant and a beautiful innocent girl, the tyrant's luxuriously decorated palace that is also full of traps, and the gang of henchmen that serves the tyrant—both oversized goons and masked assassins (in one of the most delightful scenes in Miyazaki's film, the assassins' masks come off—revealing a bunch of embarrassed, middle-aged people). The film's portrayal of Lupin himself appears to borrow both the delicate romanticism of the Chimney Sweep and the Mockingbird's talent for tricks and pranks. Fujiko's character has learned some of the Mockingbird's tricks as well—particularly toward the end of the film, when she takes over a TV news report in a manner very similar to the narration provided by the Mockingbird toward the end of Grimault's film.

As with the references to Leblanc's original novel, Miyazaki's references to Grimault's film in *The Castle of Cagliostro* show a deeper understanding of it beyond the surface-level visual and narrative similarities. Grimault's use of height and depth as metaphors is also acknowledged in Miyazaki's film: much like the evil king's castle in *The Adventures of Mr. Wonderbird*, the castle of Count Cagliostro is a similarly extravagant monument of architecture, built on the foundations of evil—the forgery operation that has been running underneath it for years, fueled not only by the Cagliostro family greed, but also by the collaboration of the nations that supported it. If Grimault presented the struggle for freedom as the struggle of the people against the tyrant, Miyazaki reminded his audience that this struggle should take place on a global, rather than personal or even national, level. In an interesting coincidence, shortly after the theatrical debut of *The Castle of Cagliostro*, Graimault won his own personal struggle for freedom: in 1980, he finally managed to complete and release his film the way he meant for it to be seen, under the new title *Le Roi el lóiseau* (*The King and the Bird*).

Most importantly, while *Puss 'n Boots* placed the basic plot structure of Grimault's film within the frame of a traditional fairy-tale, ensuring a happy ending in which the working-class boy is elevated to monarchy and lives happily ever after with the princess, *The Castle of Cagliostro* remains true to the political message of Grimault's film (even more emphasized in the 1980 version) about the need to end tyranny once and for all. Of course, this message would have been seriously diluted had Lupin taken Clarisse's offer at the end of the film and chosen to stay with her, and so *The Castle of Cagliostro* ends on a bittersweet note—despite showing throughout the film that there are more important things to fight for than greed, at the end Lupin leaves Clarisse and returns to a life of crime. As the film implies, the world needs thieves like Lupin to come to its rescue, when the authorities that are supposed to do the job cannot (global law-enforcement agencies are presented as impotent and worthless in the film, to the point that drives Zenigata to collaborate with Lupin). In this sense, the film's Lupin is not very different from many other male protagonists of other works that Miyazaki was involved with: like Ken the Wolf Boy, the Norse boy Hols and Marco, he is essentially the civilized man who comes to the jungle, saves its people, and educates them. Ironically, the "jungle" in the film is the modern political and economic system while the "civilized" man is the thief outcast.

The interpretation that Miyazaki gave Lupin's character in *The Castle of Cagliostro* was a serious departure from Katō's original manga, even more than the attempts of such interpretations in the first television series, and though this interpretation was rooted in the character's previous incarnations, it proved itself a bit too drastic for Lupin's fans. Upon its theatrical release, the film met with a lukewarm reaction at the Japanese box-office.

Outside Japan, however, where most spectators were unaware of the character's history and background, the film enjoyed a surprisingly enthusiastic response from a small but devoted crowd of fans, and many of its members would go on to become important figures in the American entertainment industry. For the non-Japanese audience who experienced a Lupin story (and Miyazaki's direction) for the first time through *The Castle of Cagliostro*, the film presented some of the most incredible action scenes ever seen, in and outside of animation. The early car-chase, the dangerous escape from the castle, and the climactic clock-tower sequence left viewers amazed. There is a persistent yet unconfirmed rumor that Steven Spielberg himself praised Miyazaki's film as adventure filmmaking at its finest (at least one DVD release of the film carried the supposed Spielberg quote on its cover).

Another important American filmmaker upon whom Miyazaki's film made a very deep impression is John Lasseter. In the early 1980s, Lasseter was a young animator at Disney, unhappy with the studio's generic productions at the time. It was the discovery of *The Castle of Cagliostro*, according to Lasseter, that demonstrated to him what animation can really do, and what kind of films he wanted to make himself. Lasseter went on to become the creative director of the computer animation studio Pixar, and his admiration for Miyazaki turned into a personal friendship between the two. He has declared that Miyazaki's movies are an important source of inspiration for the Pixar animators.[14]

Other young rising stars at Disney have also been inspired by Miyazaki's debut feature. Homage to the climactic clock-tower sequence of *The Castle of Cagliostro* was paid in the 1986 Disney feature *The Great Mouse Detective*, co-directed by John Musker, Lasseter's classmate in CalArts and later a prominent figure in Disney's renaissance of the late 1980s and early-to-mid 1990s (directing *The Little Mermaid*, *Aladdin*, and *Hercules*). Homage to the aftermath of the same sequence was also paid in another Disney film, Gary Trousdale and Kirk Wise's 2001 adventure, *Atlantis: The Lost Empire*.

The Castle of Cagliostro and Miyazaki's work in general were also an important source of inspiration for a team of young animators at the Warner Brothers Studio as they embarked on a journey to re-invent superhero animation in the early 1990s. *Batman: The Animated Series* (1991) and its many sequels and spin-offs set new standards for dark, sophisticated storytelling in American TV animation, and the animators working on them were quick to recognize Japanese animation as a rich source for ideas. An extended homage to *The Castle of Cagliostro* was paid in the climactic sequence of "The Clock King," one of the show's early episodes, with a more brief reference also made in *Batman: Mask of the Phantasm* (1993), the first feature in the animated Batman franchise. The production of *Mask of The Phantasm* also employed the services of Yukio Suzuki, a Japanese animator who started his career as an in-betweener in *The Castle of Cagliostro*, and who would go on to direct episodes of *Batman Beyond* (1999), a spectacular futuristic take on Batman's character, highly inspired by different anime shows and features.

Elementary, Lupin

While the initial poor ratings of the first television series were enough to put future plans for more animated Lupin projects on hold for several years, by the time that *The Castle of Cagliostro* debuted, the popularity of the second television series and the success of the preceding movie in the franchise were strong enough for the box-office disappointment of Miyazaki's film to have little influence on the franchise's future (in fact, new Lupin animated productions keep coming out to this very day). It did not even stop Miyazaki from having another go at directing Lupin stories, when he was invited to helm two episodes in the second television series, "Albatross, Wings of Death" and "Farewell Beloved Lupin," both broadcasted in 1980.

Both episodes are a fine example of Miyazaki's work after *The Castle of Cagliostro*: they are energetic, fast-moving, and directed with great confidence. Miyazaki was clearly thinking big after his first big-screen directorial effort, and he filled both episodes with grand action sequences. But at the same time, it appears that by this point both the small screen of television and the short timeframe of each episode began feeling like a limitation for him; each episode feels like it could have functioned well as part of a longer film, but viewed as individual pieces, they provide less than satisfactory narrative experience.

Another interesting aspect of both episodes is the heavy influence that the Superman animated cartoons produced at the Fleischer brothers' studio had on them. "Albatross, Wings of Death" pits Lupin against an evil scientist armed with nuclear bombs onboard an airplane, holding Fujiko as a hostage. The episode appears to be closely modeled on the 1942 Superman cartoon *Japoteurs*, in which Japanese spies hijack "the world's largest bombing plane" built by the American army, armed with deadly bombs and holding journalist Lois Lane as a hostage. Both *Japoteurs* and "Albatross, Wings of Death" are essentially long action sequences with paper-thin plots, but the political subtext of both is noteworthy, especially given the way that Miyazaki had managed to retain the thrills provided by the Superman film that inspired him while strongly opposing the film's theme.

Japoteurs was produced at the studio founded by the Fleischer brothers, shortly after they were forced out of it by its financiers and America had joined the war. The film is clearly a propaganda piece, with unpleasant social and racial stereotypes that Miyazaki has undoubtedly found offensive (the film presents Japanese-Americans as ugly people who are agents of Imperial Japan, scheming to harm the American war efforts), but the main point in which "Albatross, Wings of Death" goes against the film that inspires it is in the latter's celebration of military industrialism.

Fittingly for a film aimed at raising the morale of the civilians and the troops, *Japoteurs* glorifies the production of the machine in which it takes place, the advanced bomber (indeed, once the film's antagonists realize that they cannot highjack the plane, they attempt to crush this marvel of the American war industry—an act that is presented in the film as at least equally harmful). In "Albatross, Wings of Death" Miyazaki reminds his audience that for all its attractive look and features, such a bomber is actually a death machine—representing an entire industry of death (an entire assembly-line for nuclear bombs operates within the plane in the episode). This gives the episode, underneath its exciting action scenes and occasional slapstick gags, a somber tone. As in *The Castle of Cagliostro* (which gets a minor reference within "Albatross, Wings of Death" in a short scene featuring Lupin and Jigen's escape from Zenigata, which is similar to their escape from the casino at the beginning of the film), the message that Miyazaki wanted to deliver about the dangerous appeal of war machines connected with a larger political message: again, Lupin the thief is the only one who can save society from the troubles it brings upon itself.

"Farewell, Beloved Lupin" was, as its name suggests, the final episode of the series and also the last Lupin production that Miyazaki worked on. In the episode, a series of daring crimes is performed by a giant robot, and suspicion falls on Lupin's gang as the responsible party. The government, meanwhile, seems happy to exploit the situation by enforcing martial law.

"Farewell, Beloved Lupin" makes direct references to *Mechanical Monsters*, the early Superman cartoon that has already inspired several Tōei productions involving Miyazaki, as discussed in the first chapter of this book. The film and the episode have practically identical premises (a big city is terrorized by giant unstoppable robots that perform robberies) and the opening scene of the episode is almost a shot-for-shot recreation of a robbery scene from the film. *Mechanical Monsters* was produced while the Fleischer brothers were still running their studio, before the United States entered the war, and though it certainly referred to the political situation at the time it was produced, it did so in a far more elegant manner than *Japoteurs*. The film's plot about a lone scientist who lives in an isolated cave outside the big city and uses his army of remote-controlled giant robots to terrorize its citizens was a reminder to its audience (possibly motivated by the Fleischer brothers' Jewish ancestry) that while they may not feel the dangers of tyranny in faraway Europe, it is very much lurking and awaiting its prey. Unlike the xenophobic subtext of *Japoteurs*, this anti-fascist message was something that Miyazaki could identify with.

As in "Albatross, Wings of Death," Miyazaki put his own spin on the subtext of the work that inspired him. In *Mechanical Monsters*, the danger of fascism is external, representing foreign powers. In "Farewell, Beloved Lupin" this danger is internal. The government that uses the series of robberies as an excuse to oppress its own citizens is presented in the episode as at least as dangerous as the threat posed by the giant robots and their mysterious operator (a homage to Miyazaki's previous work on Tōei's *The Flying Phantom Ship*, which itself was also inspired by the Fleischers' film). Even Zenigata himself, the devoted lawman, finds the behavior of the government he serves unacceptable. And again it is Lupin the thief, the social outcast who is not a normative citizen, who saves the day.

"Farewell, Beloved Lupin" is another fine example of Miyazaki's talent for crafting grand and exciting action scenes, but it suffers from a very weak narrative structure. It features a strong, confident female character but does not give her anything really important or interesting to do and it concludes on a disappointing note with a weak twist-ending. The episode is reasonably entertaining, but it is not really at the same level of what Miyazaki has proven he can achieve with Lupin's character in *The Castle of Cagliostro*. Fortunately, though the episode was indeed Miyazaki's last Lupin story, he did manage to give the beloved thief a more fitting final bow when he adapted the stories of his grandfather's greatest literary rival.

In 1981, Miyazaki wrote and directed six episodes in the Japanese-Italian co-production "Meitantei Hōmuzu" (literally "Famous Detective Holmes," the series was titled *Sherlock Hound* in its American release), an animated adaptation of Arthur Conan Doyle's Sherlock Holmes stories, in which the entire cast was presented as anthropomorphic dogs. More action-oriented compared with Doyle's mystery-solving plots, the series nonetheless provided highly entertaining weekly thrill-rides, set against beautiful backgrounds designed in a Victorian style, with light touches of imaginary technology that refer to science fiction literature of the era.

The show's first three episodes directed by Miyazaki are an almost direct continuation of his work on the Lupin franchise in terms of story, style, and themes. In "A Small Client," Holmes is approached by a little girl who asks him to find her lost cat. Though the episode opens with a terrific sequence reminiscent of Holmes' literary roots, in which he deciphers an encoded message, it soon changes direction into an equally entertaining action affair as the hero has to put a stop to his rival Moriarty's plan to flood Britain with forged coins. The now-familiar plot about forged money from *The Castle of Cagliostro* and even earlier episodes of the first Lupin television series does not quite carry the same political subtext it did before—perhaps because Holmes, unlike Lupin,

Featuring many plot-elements familiar from Miyazaki's work on *Lupin III*, only now from the law-enforcing side, the director's work on *Sherlock Hound* served as a farewell to the famous thief.

works with the law rather than against it—but it provides the episode with a very satisfying climax and conclusion.

Fun continued with the following episode, "Mrs. Hudson Is Taken Hostage," in which Holmes' housekeeper is kidnapped by Moriarty in an attempt to extort Holmes into stealing the Mona Lisa from the London National Gallery (loaned by the Louvre, one assumes). The episode plays almost like a piece of fan-fiction: what would Holmes do if he had found himself in Lupin's shoes? The setup for the episode's robbery scene includes a classic Lupin-style threatening letter sent to the police, an angry Inspector Lestrade who could double for Zenigata, and a clever deception trick that would have made Lupin proud. It all adds up to a highly entertaining story that becomes even more entertaining with hilarious scenes portraying Moriarty and his henchmen as they attempt to deal with their hostage. These scenes even portray Moriarty in a somewhat sympathetic light—one particularly amusing sequence has him daydreaming about having a proper family household with Mrs. Hudson as his wife, though he cannot quite separate such a "proper" life from his career as a criminal, even in his fantasies. In this sense, it was not only Holmes but also Moriarty who becomes a version of Lupin in the episode, in a sense inheriting the famous thief's tragic nature of being doomed to a life of crime.

The third Miyazaki episode of the show, "The Blue Ruby" (the name alludes to the literary Holmes mystery, *The Adventure of The Blue Carbuncle*, though the episode almost unrelated to it otherwise), opens with Moriarty pulling a clever Lupin-like stunt of his own, when he creates a large-scale diversion in order to steal a precious gemstone. But shortly afterwards he loses it to a young, resourceful pickpocket girl—who soon must rely on Holmes to pull herself out of trouble. Much like Miyazaki's work on the Lupin franchise, this episode carries the sentiment that not all thieves are bad people.

The following episode, "Treasure under the Sea" has Holmes foiling another scheme by Moriarty, this time to use an advanced submarine in order to rob a recently discovered underwater treasure. The real stars of the episode, however, are the different pieces of machinery seen throughout—especially Moriarty's submarine (which he constructs himself, using parts stolen from the navy) and a small airplane-airship used by Holmes to track him. In a sense, both machines represent the rebellious nature of both characters. Moriarty uses the submarine to commit crimes, yet it is hard not to appreciate the way he outsmarts the navy's big ships and large crew; similarly, Holmes manages to track down Moriarty using his hastily constructed flying machine, while the army, equipped with more advanced devices, fails to do so. Both examples bring to mind Lupin's innovative use of technologies, set against the clumsy, often corrupt, and sometimes downright stupid nature of large organizations such as the government and the army and their unimaginative assembly-line production processes.

The fifth episode directed by Miyazaki, "The White Cliffs of Dover," also celebrated individual pioneering of technology. Moriarty's scheme this time around concerns an attempt to sabotage airplanes and shut down the country's air-mail service. Holmes comes to the aid of air-mail pilots, who must put together, maintain, and repair their airplanes on their own, making their machines particularly vulnerable to Moriarty's attacks. The real hero of the episode, however, turns out to be Mrs. Hudson—the widow of one of the country's greatest aviation pioneers, who makes it her mission to secure the future of the air-mail service and the heritage of her late husband. It is Mrs. Hudson, rather than Holmes, who strikes the final blow against Moriarty's operation.

"The White Cliffs of Dover" is the most spectacular among the episodes directed by Miyazaki in the show: a large chunk of it is devoted to exciting sky and car chases that bring to mind both "Albatross, Wings of Death" and "The Castle of Cagliostro." At the same time, the subplot concerning Mrs. Hudson's past brings a stronger emotional subtext to the episode compared with the rest of the show. It is the best episode that Miyazaki has directed for the show, and one of the peaks of his television career.

Miyazaki's final episode of the show, "Where Did the Sovereigns Go?", brings characters back to their traditional roles—Holmes is the logic-driven detective who solves the mystery almost immediately after being introduced to it; Moriarty is the master-thief who performs a daring robbery (which bears more than a passing resemblance to Lupin's capers). But the episode also carries a much stronger political subtext compared with its predecessors. The story follows Holmes' investigation into the disappearance of a small amount of money from the protected high-tech safe of a wealthy industrialist. Though Holmes deducts the culprit's method quickly, discovering its identity is another matter, as suspects are not hard to come by—the industrialist practically owns the entire town that resides underneath his luxurious castle, and all of the town's residents live in poverty, with a deep grudge against him.

"Where Did the Sovereigns Go?" is strongly inspired by *The Adventures of Mr. Wonderbird*, and much like *The Castle of Cagliostro* this influence is most apparent in the episode's metaphoric use of height and depth to indicate class differences—again, a wealthy, pompous (though this time around, not necessarily evil) man lives in a luxurious castle, high above the poor common folk. More direct visual references include the design of the industrialist's castle, reminiscent of the architecture of the tyrant's palace in *The Adventures of Mr. Wonderbird*, and the industrialist's safe, designed as a grotesque statue made in his image, not unlike the many grotesque monuments that adorn the tyrant's kingdom in Grimault's film. Even the industrialist's pet bird is somewhat similar to the Mockingbird in the film.

As with the show's other episodes, "Where Did the Sovereigns Go?" skillfully leads its audience through a captivating story, yet it ends on a somewhat sudden note—for a moment, it appears that the industrialist has understood the negative consequences of his greed, but a moment later, he is again fighting to regain his lost money. There is no real sign that the town's people are any better off than they were before when Holmes bids them farewell. It is something of a downbeat conclusion to Miyazaki's work on the show, demonstrating how it is not always possible to solve all the world's problems with either a detective or a thief.

Miyazaki directed the six episodes of *Sherlock Hound* in 1981, but legal complications with Arthur Conan Doyle's estate held back their broadcast until 1984—the year in which Miyazaki's theatrical feature *Nausicaa of the Valley of the Wind* debuted. The feature's success effectively ended the director's long television career, marking his final move to theatrical features.[15]

Notes

1   Frederik L. Schodt, *Dreamland Japan: Writings on Modern Manga* (Berkeley: Stone Bridge Press, 1996), 49–53.
2   Fred Patten, *Watching Anime, Reading Manga*, 240.
3   See George Kelly, "Caper," and T.J. Binson, "Gentleman Thief" in *The Oxford Companion to Crime and Mystery Writing*, eds. Rosemary Herbert, Catherine Aird, John M. Reilly, and Susan Oleksiw (Oxford: Oxford University Press), 55–56; 180.
4   See Jacques Baudou, "Lupin, Arsene," and Kate Bengal, "Theft" in *The Oxford Companion to Crime and Mystery Writing*, eds. Rosemary Herbert, Catherine Aird, John M. Reilly and Susan Oleksiw (Oxford: Oxford University Press), 273; 456–457.
5   See, for example, the very first volume of Lupin the Third's stories: Monkey Punch, *Lupin III Vol. 1* (Los Angeles: Tokyopop, 2002).

6   Miyazaki, *Starting Point*, 277–283.
7   From the liner notes written on the pilot film by Reed Nelson, included
    with the R1 DVD release of the show by Discotek Media in 2012.
8   See the article "Trains and Scalps" by Daniel Thomas MacInnes, included
    with the R1 DVD release of the show by Discotek Media in 2012.
9   Neither director, in fact, received credit for his work on the show; while the
    pre-Miyazaki and Takahata episodes were credited to director Masaaki
    Ōsumi (who also worked on the pilot), the direction of the episodes
    helmed by the new creative team was credited to "A Production" (the
    studio that employed Miyazaki and Takahata at the time). Reed Nelson
    speculates that at least some influence, and perhaps even some hands-on
    work by Osumi, can still be traced to the early episodes directed by
    Miyazaki and Takahata. See the liner notes and the television series credits
    included with the R1 DVD release of the show by Discotek Media in 2012.
10 All English episode titles are taken from the R1 DVD release of the show
    by Discotek Media in 2012.
11 McCarthy, *Hayao Miyazaki, Master of Japanese Animation*, 53.
    Interestingly, acclaimed French filmmaker Francois Truffaut has found
    strong parallels between Hitchcock's film and Leblanc's original Lupin
    novels, treating *To Catch a Thief* as a far superior interpretation of
    Leblanc's Lupin than the official 1957 French film adaptation of Leblanc's
    novels in his book *The Films in My Life* (New York: Da Capo Press, 1994),
    80–81, 180–183.
12 Maurice Leblanc, *The Memoirs of Arsene Lupin* (New York: The Macaulay
    Company, 1925).
13 McCarthy, *Hayao Miyazaki, Master of Japanese Animation*, 53.
14 Miyazaki, *Starting Point*, 9–10.
15 This chapter, especially in the section concerning *The Castle of Cagliostro*,
    is based and expands on a feature by me: "An Auteur is Born: 30 Years of
    Hayao Miyazaki's Castle of Cagliostro," originally published in 2009 at the
    Animated Views website. Available online: http://animatedviews.
    com/2009/an-auteur-is-born-30-years-of-miyazakis-castle-of-cagliostro/

Chapter 4

TO THE VALLEY BELOW

Although *The Castle of Cagliostro* was not an instant success upon its release, the film did draw the attention of prominent figures in the animation industry, and as well as getting enthusiastic responses from foreign viewers (as detailed in the previous chapter) it also made a strong impression on the editors of the Japanese magazine *Animage*. Founded in 1978 as a serious platform for the discussion of animated productions, while at the same time appealing to the now-established and ever growing fandom of animation in Japan, the magazine commissioned articles and sketches from Miyazaki, and in 1981 the editors agreed to serialize a long-running manga drawn by him (there are conflicting reports as to the circumstances that led to the publication of the manga, discussed further in this chapter).[1] The series, *Kaze no Tani no Naushika* (*Nausicaa of the Valley of the Wind*) aimed from the beginning to be a long and complex work; its first chapter was published in the magazine in 1982 and its concluding chapter was published 12 years and over a thousand pages of story later, with occasional long hiatuses taken by Miyazaki to work on animated features.

The series is set in a post-apocalyptic world in which humanity has regressed into pseudo-medieval society, struggling for its survival as it must co-exist with The Sea of Decay—a huge toxic forest that emits poisonous miasma into the atmosphere, populated with mutated insects and giant Ohmu worms.

Yet even such a harsh existence does not prevent the different human kingdoms from waging war on each other, using deadly weapon-technology inherited from the days before the apocalyptic "Seven Days of Fire." Two main powers struggle for domination: the militant kingdom of Torumekia, somewhat reminiscent of the Roman Empire, and the Dorok Empire, a tribal society ruled by religious priests. Peaceful lands are caught in the struggle—the series begins when an ancient powerful

Inspired by science fiction literature and film, the world of *Nausicaa of the Valley of the Wind* is one where nature dwarfs mankind, making its presence in the world less and less significant as time passes.

weapon is discovered in the industrial city of Pejite, and as a result the city is invaded and destroyed by Kushana, princess and ruthless leader of the Torumekian army. Refugees from Pejite attempt to make their way to another peaceful kingdom, the Valley of the Wind, set at the edge of The Sea of Decay.

The Valley of the Wind is led by the aging and dying King Jhil, whose beautiful daughter Nausicaa is renowned for her pacifism and strong belief that humankind can co-exist with the dwellers of the forest. Kushana arrives at the Valley to hunt down the remaining survivors from Pejite, and soon enough crosses paths with Nausicaa. But since the Valley of the Wind is a military ally of Torumekia, Nausicaa has little choice but to join Kushana in the latter's conquest campaign.

Throughout this campaign, however, Nausicaa proves herself to be highly devoted to her mission to end wars, violence, and the continuous destruction of nature by mankind. Witnessing her leadership by example, many other characters—notably the vengeful prince Asbel of Pejite, the high ranking commander-priest of the Dorok army Chruka, and eventually Kushana herself—are won over by Nausicaa's pacifism. And, as Nausicaa discovers, the toxic environment that dominated the world has its own purpose, and humans have a role to fulfill in it. It is just unclear whether this role will bring their salvation or extinction.

Nausicaa of the Valley of the Wind is a triumph. It is a sweeping tale of epic proportions that presents an incredibly rich futuristic world populated with unforgettable characters and weaves together a complex and captivating tale that is occasionally brutal but also deeply humane. This story is deeply rooted in works that influenced Miyazaki, discussed in depth throughout this chapter, but its two most direct creative ancestors were produced by Miyazaki himself.

Nausicaa of the Valley of the Wind was not Miyazaki's first foray into manga drawing. He had previously published (under a pseudonym) manga adaptations of both the *Puss 'n Boots* and *Animal Treasure Island* films that he worked on during his time at Tōei. His first significant work as a manga artist, however, was *Sabaku no Tami* (*People of the Desert*) serialized between 1969 and 1970 in a children's newspaper.[2]

The series takes place against the historical backdrop of Central Asia in the eleventh century, albeit in the fictional land of the Soqute clan of nomads, whose people face an invasion by the militant clan of the Kittarl. The series follows a young Soqute boy named Tem who witnesses his father's death at the hands of Kittarl warriors after giving shelter to a fellow Soqute fugitive. Tem goes on a journey to avenge his father's death, and with friends he makes along the way—a boy named Tahn and a girl named Sasan—aids the Soqute people in their struggle to free their capital Pejite from the oppressive Kittarl.

Several elements from *People of the Desert* resurface later in *Nausicaa of the Valley of the Wind*: like Miyazaki's later work, it is a tale of struggle and conquest, involving an aggressive militant power showing how such struggles have a tragic effect on people's lives, especially young people. The brutality of war as it is portrayed in *People of the Desert* is particularly echoed in *Nausicaa of the Valley of the Wind*: in two memorable (and quite disturbing, considering that the series was aimed at young readers) scenes, Tem sees his friends killed by Kittarl soldiers.

People of the Desert itself is inspired by Miyazaki's previous works and by the works that influenced him. Fukushima's *Devil of the Desert* inspired the exotic backdrop of desert landscapes that are foreign to Miyazaki's native Japan, where a threat of apocalyptic nature arises. Of course, Miyazaki has used this setting in a far more serious and somber tone, replacing the supernatural threat and exciting adventures from Fukushima's manga with the grim historical backdrop of a tragic war. Miyazaki's own work on *The Little Norse Prince* provided a strong narrative background for *People of the Desert*—again, the story of a boy who unifies an entire community in a struggle against an oppressor, and much like the residents of the town in Takahata's film, the Soqute people in Miyazaki's manga are initially frightened, suspicious, and even willing to turn against other members of their own clan to ensure their survival. And like Hols before him, Tem is the "civilized" child who educated the people of the "jungle" in their struggle against oppression.

Like *The Little Norse Prince, People of the Desert* features many early elements that would become the hallmarks of Miyazaki's later acclaimed works, but in comparison with these works, it is underdeveloped and immature. When compared with *Nausicaa of the Valley of the Wind*, in particular, *People of the Desert* features inferior art (characters have sketchy design and landscapes are very low on detail) and feels like a juvenile story—while Tem's "education" of his people amounts to uniting them in a fight against their enemy, Nausicaa teaches the people of her world about the futility of war and the importance of the preservation of nature. There are also no true antagonists or truly bad people in *Nausicaa of the Valley of the Wind*: characters have their faults and they sometimes surrender to their selfish impulses, but almost everyone eventually repents.

The second early work by Miyazaki that paved the way to *Nausicaa of the Valley of the Wind*, on the other hand, can be considered as his first true masterpiece. In 1978, Miyazaki wrote and directed *Mirai Shōnen Conan (Future Boy Conan)*, a 13-hour epic television series spread across 26 episodes. The series loosely adapts *The Incredible Tide*, a novel by American author Alexander Key (probably best-known today as the author of another science fiction novel, *Escape to Witch Mountain*, which has been successfully adapted several times by Disney).[3] Miyazaki gave the source material his own unique touch, and it could be considered as the first solid appearance of his personal style, familiar to the audience of his films today. Compared with Miyazaki's previous directorial efforts—the *Yuki's Sun* pilot, the *Lupin the Third* episodes he co-helmed with Takahata, and even his first solo feature as director *The Castle of Cagliostro* that came out a year later—*Future Boy Conan* features far more complex themes and plotting, and it can be said to have truly pushed Miyazaki's work to the next level.

The show takes place after a nuclear war that left the world in ruins. Its protagonist, Conan, is an 11-year-old boy who lives with his grandfather on an isolated island. His grandfather is the last survivor of a failed attempt to flee the planet using a rocket that crash-landed on the island. The happy and curious Conan, who seems to have an almost supernatural strength, spends most of his time fishing. As the story begins, a mysterious girl named Lana, who is the same age as Conan, is washed up on the shores of the island. As it soon turns out, Lana plays an important role in the struggle between the two leading powers in the world—the militant city of Industria and the utopian community of High Harbor. During their voyage, Conan and Lana are joined by a fat and somewhat selfish boy named Jimsy. Their adventures will re-shape the world they live in.

Throughout the first half of the show, most of the episodes confront the protagonists with agents of Industria. Here Miyazaki reveals his gift for characterization that will feel so familiar to fans of his later works: most of these agents are not one-dimensional villains, but people who act out of a belief in what Industria stands for. Especially memorable is the character of Monsley, a determined officer in the ranks of Industria, who in the course of the show becomes a character almost as central as the other protagonists. A more humorous approach is represented by the character of Captain Dyce, a greedy mercenary-sailor in the service of Industria, who also goes through a deep change in the course of the show.

The design of Industria is heavily inspired by Grimault's *The Adventures of Mr. Wonderbird*. The metaphor of height in Grimault's film, previously referenced by Miyazaki in *The Castle of Cagliostro*, is again used in *Future Boy Conan* for the same purpose: the rulers of Industria reside in the upper levels of its high towers, while the slaves who work on its assembly-lines live in underground tunnels. Miyazaki also borrowed a few ideas from his work on *The Flying Ghost Ship* in the series' portrayal of Industria, notably a council of scientists that manage the city. The trio of protagonists, consisting of two boys and a girl who find themselves in the middle of a military conflict somewhat echoes Miyazaki's work on *People of the Desert*.

Around halfway into the show's continuous plot, when the protagonists reach High Harbor, it goes through a change in its atmosphere. The action sequences that dominated the first half of the show make way for a coming-of-age drama about the difficulties of Conan and Jimsy—who both learned to rely only on themselves in the struggle for survival—to fit within the peaceful and ideal society they find themselves in. It is a hard process, and it can be argued that eventually they fail to find their place in this community, and this failure gives a bitter feeling to the later parts of the show. The show's message about the ability of the younger generation to build a better world than the one ruined by their parents also applies to High Harbor: despite the ideal living in this community, it is not a perfect place, and its flaws are revealed as the plot progresses.

Though the design of High Harbor may seem a little out-of-place at first—a pastoral European village in the middle of a ruined world—there is logic behind this design choice. Miyazaki's design of High Harbor shows a strong influence of the European landscapes of the kind that he researched for the *Calpis/World Masterpiece Theatre* productions, where such landscapes often provided the backdrop for coming-of-age stories, with the passage from one location to another serving as a metaphor for growing up, as it serves in Conan and Jimsy's story.

The closing episodes of the show bring the conflict between Industria and High Harbor to its climax and return the show to its action-driven plot. Then the show ends—and as always in a Miyazaki story, the end brings the promise of a new beginning. Not all of the world's problems are over, but the ending of *Future Boy Conan* promises that they can be solved.

The show has some shortcomings, mostly in its visual design. Though it had a larger budget than most TV anime productions of its era, and though Miyazaki was a far more talented director than many of his colleagues, certain limitations in both design and animation can still be felt throughout the show. The most obvious is in the characters—for some reason, for most of the episodes all characters appear to suffer from a bad case of strabismus. The over-dramatic music is also not up to the level of the wonderful scores provided by Hisaishi Joe for Miyazaki's later films.

But despite these shortcomings, Miyazaki created in the show a wonderfully detailed world and its 13-hour story allowed him to explore it to depths that would have been impossible in a two-hour film (scenes from different episodes of the show were edited in 1984 into a theatrical feature, without Miyazaki's involvement and to an unimpressive result). Very often, in the middle of a plot that storms breathlessly from one location to the other, the show suddenly comes to a halt and closely examines another detail or aspect of everyday life in the harsh world in which it takes place. Miyazaki leads his audience across the world with the confidence of a gifted storyteller.

Perhaps the strongest evidence to the importance of the show in the Miyazaki canon is the huge influence it had on his future works. *Nausicaa of the Valley of the Wind* is probably the closest work to the show, at least thematically: both works deal with the ecological implications of human behavior on the world. Both works also present the idea that the world can renew and regenerate itself from the damage caused by the same behavior.

Both works feature a protagonist who—in what now became a familiar trope in Miyazaki's works—is a "civilized" young person who educates the people surrounding him about how to build a better society. A more specific influence is the character of Monsley—who feels like a combination of the two rival princesses from Miyazaki's later work: Nausicaa and Kushana. Monsley has Kushana's ruthlessness and tyrannical attitude, but also Nausicaa's determination and sense of justice. The design of her character also inspired elements in both later characters: though Monsly's facial design is closer to Kushana's, her flaming-red hair is more reminiscent of Nausicaa's.

Future Boy Conan remains an important milestone in Miyazaki's career that is unfortunately not familiar enough to his fans in the English-speaking world; at the time of writing, no English-subbed or dubbed version of the show is available commercially.

The Heroine's Journey

While *Future Boy Conan* provided inspiration for key elements in *Nausicaa of the Valley of the Wind*, it was also a very male-oriented show with the protagonist being, as noted earlier, the archetypical Miyazaki "civilized" boy who educates the people around him. Lana's character in the show feels bland and underdeveloped, serving as little more than a plot device; Monsley is a far more complex character, but she also largely serves as a supporting character for Conan. *Nausicaa of the Valley of the Wind*, on the other hand, focuses on a female protagonist and has been praised by different critics for providing a positive role model of a strong leading female figure for his readers.[4] In fact, Miyazaki's tendency to place female characters in dominant roles in his works can be traced to *Nausicaa of the Valley of the Wind*. Nausicaa's character, however, was inspired by many previous works that Miyazaki was involved with, and other works he read or watched in the two decades that passed between the beginning of his professional career and the publication of the first chapter of the manga.

The initial inspiration for Nausicaa's character came from the protagonists of two ancient literary sources. One was the protagonist of *The Lady who Loved Insects*, a story by an unknown author from the Japanese collection *Tsutsumi Chūnagon Monogatari* ("The Riverside Middle Counselor's Tales") originally published during the late Heian (795–1185 CE) period. The Heian period was a time of economic prosperity leading to cultural flourishing and the writing of many literary classics. Though the author of *The Lady who Loved Insects* is unknown, the story's ironic tone implies that the intent behind it was to satirize the popular subject matter of many literary works of the period—the life of nobility.[5]

The story's unnamed protagonist is the daughter of a noble family who refuses to conform to social norms, especially those concerned with beauty. Though she is a beautiful woman, she refuses to pluck her eyebrows, blacken her teeth, or trim her hair as fashion dictates. Instead, she devotes her time to her greatest passion—collecting and studying "all kinds of reptiles and insects, such as most people are frightened to touch," especially caterpillars. The strange hobby reflects the lady's desire for knowledge and understanding of the world, her wish to see the inner works underneath the superficiality of social life: "I want to inquire into everything that exists, and find out how it began ... it is very silly of them to dislike caterpillars, all of which will soon turn into lovely butterflies." While people of the social circles that surround the lady are largely appalled by her behavior, she manages to gather a group of boys who help her collect insects. Toward the end of the story, the lady also captures the attention of a nobleman who finds her odd behavior attractive. The story ends with a hint of courtship and a promise of a continuation in the "next scroll," though the rest of the story, if ever written, has been lost.

The second literary heroine that inspired Miyazaki, and gave the protagonist of the manga her name, is Nausicaa from Homer's *Odyssey*. A princess of the island of Phaeacia, who became renowned for her beauty, Homer's Nausicaa met Odysseus when he washed up on the shore of her island, unconscious. Unlike the frightened reaction of her handmaidens, Nausicaa demonstrated resourcefulness at the sight of the man, bringing him to safety and tending to his wounds, eventually saving his life. Nausicaa's parents were displeased with the appearance of the mysterious man on their shore, at first worried about a prophecy concerning a stranger who tells tall tales and later, when they find out the true identity of their guest, about their daughter's growing affection for Odysseus (knowing that he has a wife waiting for him). With urging from Nausicaa's parents, Odysseus eventually leaves the island, leaving Nausicaa behind, heartbroken.

Miyazaki first read about Nausicaa in *Gods, Demigods and Demons*, a reference book for Greek Mythology written for young readers by American author Bernard Evslin. The entry devoted to Nausicaa in

Evslin's book is rich, detailed, and longer than most other entries, including that of Odysseus himself.[6] Evslin vividly describes Nausicaa as a strong, resourceful, and independent woman, who is also of legendary beauty and possesses a special talent for poetry and singing. More important, perhaps, is the reason given by Evslin for Nausicaa's rejection of her many suitors: "She wanted a man whose wit was as quick as hers and who would have her same vivid response to things that others overlooked." Like the protagonist of *The Lady who Loved Insects*, Evslin describes Homer's Nausicaa as a bright girl who looks deeper, beyond the superficial.

Many of the elements that Miyazaki borrowed from both the heroine of classic Japanese literature and the heroine of Greek mythology in the creation of his manga are easy to spot. Miyazaki's Nausicaa possesses a great love of nature and is strongly attracted to forest creatures that other people find repulsive, notably the giant Ohmu, not unlike the fascination that the lady from the Japanese tale expresses toward caterpillars; the band of boys that the protagonist of the Japanese legend gathers as followers also parallels the growing number of characters—men and women—who are enlightened by her beliefs. Homer's/Evslin's Nausicaa gave Miyazaki's heroine her name, her beauty, and her strong resourceful personality, along with her compassion for the wounded and sick. The ambiguous manner in which both the unknown author of *The Lady who Loved Insects* and Homer/Evslin leave readers guessing about the fate of their heroines (the Japanese story, as noted above, ends with a promise of continuation never fulfilled while Evslin provides several conflicting stories of Nausicaa's fate after her farewell from Odysseus, noting that there is an uncertainty about which, if any, is true) also influenced Miyazaki, who at the concluding page of the manga also briefly reports of conflicting "legends" about his heroine's fate.

The traits that made both literary heroines so influential on Miyazaki's Nausicaa can also be found in other heroines that he came across in other projects that he worked on. The protagonists of both *Heidi, Girl of the Alps* and *Anne of Green Gables* have also shown a great love for nature alongside a strong independent character that sometimes brought them into direct conflict with the norms of "proper" society. Another inspiration may have come from the very first animated heroine that inspired Miyazaki to seek a career in animation—Bai-Niang, the heroine of *Panda and the Magic Serpent*, who openly rebels against the social norms that forbid the love between her and the scholar Xu-Xian.

But there is an element that existed in all three heroines, and to a certain extent also in the heroines of *The Lady who Loved Insects* and in

Homer's/Evslin's Nausicaa, which does not exist in Miyazaki's Nausicaa: eventually, all these characters that inspired Miyazaki's Nausicaa find a way to fit in with the society that surrounds them while maintaining their independent personality and channeling this personality for the benefit of this society. In Miyazaki's manga, this is mostly a one-sided process: Nausicaa never integrates into the human society that surrounds her, but rather changes and shapes this society in the image of her ideals. She has nothing to learn from the human society of the post-apocalyptic world that surrounds her, she can only teach. This gives Nausicaa's character a certain feeling of one-dimensionality; unlike the characters that inspired her, Miyazaki's heroine does not develop or grow in the course of the story because she has nowhere and nothing to grow into, she is already perfect. Scholar Susan Napier even went as far as describing Nausicaa as "boring."[7]

Nowhere is this lack of development of Miyazaki's Nausicaa felt more strongly than in the character's attitude—or lack thereof—toward the opposite sex. Of the characters that inspired her, the protagonist of *The Lady who Loved Insects* ends her story with a hint of upcoming romance between her and the man who became fascinated with her unusual behavior; Homer's/Evslin's Nausicaa is said to have found love after Odysseus left her, either in Odysseus' son or a blind poet; and a part of Anne's integration into society is admitting that she has feelings for Gilbert Blythe. In Miyazaki's manga, Nausicaa shows no romantic interest in any character whatsoever. Despite her beauty, the character is presented throughout the series as asexual.

Nausicaa's asexuality does not, by itself, make her character less complex. But it does point to a certain aspect in which she places herself above normative society in her world, in a rather patronizing manner: though she shows great affection toward children and old people, Nausicaa appears to reject the notion of family, not just for herself but for others as well. Nausicaa idealizes harmony among human beings and pacifism, but not the family social structure. As readers find out in the course of the series, this attitude can be traced to the role models that Nausicaa had in her own childhood: her father, King Jhil, was a kind person but also a sickly, weak, and ineffective leader (Nausicaa found a much better father figure in Yupa, the sword-master who trained her, and she obviously sees him as a stronger role model than her own biological father); her mother was a cold and distant woman, incapable of loving her own child. It is perhaps for this reason that one of the few occasions in the series where Nausicca fails is when she becomes a mother herself—adopting the monstrous "God Warrior," a sentient weapon left from the war that ruined the world. Nausicaa develops a deep emotional connection with the creature, but eventually leads it to sacrifice itself as part of her mission to save the world.

This negative view of the notion of family may have originated in another work that inspired Miyazaki's Nausicaa, a work far less literary ambitious compared with any of those discussed so far. In 1980, Miyazaki wrote a proposal for an animated feature adaptation of the comic series *Rowlf* by American artist Richard Corben.[8] Originally published in 1971 in an underground magazine, the series tells the story of a princess in a peaceful kingdom, who is always accompanied by her loyal dog Rowlf. Her aging father is looking for a man to marry her, and she is courted by a mean, stupid prince, whom Rowlf deeply dislikes. One day, after bathing in a lake, the princess is kidnapped by an army of demons. Rowlf, unable to stop the demons, is at first accused of killing the princess. In an attempt to find out what happened, a wizard casts a spell that is supposed to turn Rowlf into a human, but the spell goes wrong— leaving Rowlf half-man-half-beast. In his new shape, Rowlf can now go and save the princess.[9]

Corben, who started his career in the American underground comics scene of the 1960s, gained fame for drawing science fiction, fantasy, and horror stories with strong erotic content. *Rowlf* features many of the elements that made Corben's work famous—a violent fantasy setting with exploitive nudity thrown in for good measure—and judged on its own merits, it is not an exceptional work in either story or art. The fantasy story feels generic and clichéd, character designs are sometimes badly proportioned, almost all characters look hideously ugly, and throughout the story Corben seems to have a problem fitting the text into boxes and speech balloons, which often results in an uncomfortable reading experience.

Miyazaki's proposed adaptation of the series changes a key element in the story—Rowlf is not turned into a man-beast creature after a spell is cast on him, but rather as a result of his longing for his mistress. Sketches that Miyazaki prepared for the adaptation reveal that he also intended to emphasize another element that in Corben's original story was practically non-existent—the princess' father who is presented as an old, sickly, and inefficient ruler.[10] This character appears in only a single panel in the original comics, with no dialogue of its own; in Miyazaki's proposed adaptation, the princess' relationship with her father was supposed to be a major plotline.

Though Miyazaki's proposal for the adaptation of *Rowlf* was rejected, this plotline found its way to *Nausicaa of the Valley of the Wind* as is evident in Nausicaa's own relationship with her father—who is also an old, sickly, and ineffective ruler. This relationship is also symbolic of the post-apocalyptic setting of the series—the elders leave their children a ruined world, and the children must forgo the old ways of their parents to rebuild it. The unflattering manner in which Corben presents the princess' suitor in *Rowlf*, and the princess' eventual rejection of him, also echoes in Nausicaa's asexuality: romantic relationship, and the wish to bring up another generation of children, are also a custom of the "old world" (especially for a royal heiress) that Nausicaa does not wish to take part in. And despite the unattractive style, minor visual influences of Corben's comics can also be spotted in Miyazaki's manga: the use of modern military technology in a pseudo-medieval environment by the demons in *Rowlf* recalls the use of mechanized vehicles in the post-apocalyptic world that features many medieval elements in *Nausicaa of the Valley of the Wind* (especially in the portrayal of the Torumekian military) and throughout *Rowlf* Corben draws some highly effective action-oriented pages with no text, which appear to have somewhat influenced the way that Miyazaki handles action scenes in his own comics.

Nausicaa is not the only significant female character in the series. The Torumekian princess Kushana is almost every bit a protagonist of the manga and in many ways serves as a dark mirror for Nausicaa: like Nausicaa, Kushana is a skilled warrior and natural leader. But while Nausicaa wins the admiration of her followers through compassion, Kushana leads through ruthlessness and fear. This can of course be attributed to the different backgrounds both characters came from (Nausicaa is the princess of a peaceful kingdom while Kushana is the princess of a militant empire) but also to the families that the characters grew in: the cold and distant approach of Nausicaa's mother made Nausicaa spread love and compassion to all those who surround her, perhaps as compensation for what she herself did not have, while Kushana witnessed how her emotional and loving mother was not fit for life in the cruel world that surrounded her, turning Kushana herself into a tough and ruthless person. Kushana's background appears to have been inspired by a character from another work that strongly influenced Miyazaki—the Snow Queen from Lev Atamanov's film. The two characters portray the same ruthlessness toward the people who surround them, and even share a similar look (especially in the facial design, and the robes that the Snow Queen wears also echo somewhat in Kushana's clothing). But while the Snow Queen was a generic villain in Atamanov's film, evil for the sake of being evil, Miyazaki gave Kushana a strong background, which explains her behavior.

Another significant female character in Miyazaki's manga is the wise old woman of the Valley of the Wind—an oracle and keeper of lore. This character features mostly in the early chapters of the manga, yet she plays an important role: as a person who saw, throughout her long life, the many atrocities that mankind is capable of, her wisdom and experience are highly valued by the people of the valley and Nausicaa in particular. The wise old woman character also appears to be inspired by similar characters of old women from Atamanov's film who aid the protagonist in her quest.

Like Nausicaa, Kushana shows no romantic or sexual interest in men (the only segment in which she considers taking a spouse is when the option of her political marriage to the monstrous Dorok Emperor arises—an option that, fortunately for Kushana, does not last long), and there is no indication in the series that the wise old woman ever had children of her own in her youth. The women who shape the fate of the world in the series appear to realize that this world is just too cruel to bring new life into.

The Forbidden Paradise

The initial inspiration for the post-apocalyptic setting of *Nausicaa of the Valley of the Wind* came from a real environmental incident. In the mid-to-late 1950s, a neurological epidemic broke out in the Japanese city of Minamata. The disease affected the victims' ability to move and talk and claimed the lives of over 1,500 people. Investigations have revealed that the cause of the disease was industrial waste poured into the water of the city's bay, leading to mercury poisoning, which found its way to the fish in many of the residents' meals. The "Minamata Disease" led to growing awareness of environmental issues among the Japanese public and encouraged the Japanese government to take action on such issues.[11] Miyazaki, however, was inspired by what appeared to be nature's own reaction: fear of the disease has led to a decline and eventual stopping of fishing in the area, and this in turn has led to a sharp increase in the fish population at the bay's water. Upon learning this fact, Miyazaki felt awed by the ability of nature to preserve itself in the face of human behavior.[12]

In a key scene in *Nausicaa of the Valley of the Wind*, the heroine discovers that there is a purpose behind the toxic air pollution caused by the giant "Sea of Decay" forest: it cleanses the Earth with the aim of making it habitable again. But will mankind survive the process?

The world of *Nausicaa of the Valley of the Wind*, in which giant forests cleanse the Earth by absorbing poison from the soil and releasing it into the air, creating an environment where giant insects and arthropods can exist while the same is not necessarily true for human beings, is also a world where nature outlasts the human race.

Additional inspiration for such a world came from several renowned works of science fiction. The most prominent example is *Hothouse*, a novel by British writer Brian Aldiss published in 1962. Like Miyazaki's manga, Aldiss' book also describes a world in which the age of man has passed. Plants that became sentient beings now rule the planet, dwarfing the few surviving humans whose lives are a constant struggle. Though the world of *Hothouse* has reached its state not though the actions of human beings but due to changes in planetary conditions, it delivers the same sense of a place where the human race is slowly dying and heading on its way to becoming a distant memory while new life forms evolve and take over.[13] The opening chapter of the book also presents the readers with a very Nausicaa-like heroine named Lily-yo, the strong leader of a small human community. Though Lily-yo's decision of abandoning older members of her tribe as they make survival for the rest of the community impossible is something that Miyazaki's heroine probably wouldn't have done (the manga emphasizes the great respect she shows toward older figures), the need to make hard decisions in the face of a harsh reality is certainly something that both the protagonist of Miyazaki's manga and Aldiss' book have in common.

Another environmentally themed science fiction novel that strongly echoes in Miyazaki's manga is Frank Herbert's *Dune*, published in 1965 and long considered one of the genre's greatest masterpieces. The novel takes place in the distant future on the planet Arrakis, a desert-world that is the only source in the universe of spice—a life-prolonging drug that is also vital for interplanetary travel. The plot opens as the idealistic noble house of Atreides is put in charge of spice-mining on the planet, but members of the house are soon betrayed by the Emperor who sent them, and the militant rival house of Harkonnen. While almost all the house's members are massacred, its young heir Paul and his mother Jessica escape to the harsh wilderness of the planet and find refuge among the Fremen, a wandering tribe of tough warriors who have made the deadly desert planet their home. Paul becomes a leader and a messianic figure among the Fremen, eventually leading them in a military campaign against the Emperor and the house of Harkonnen, reclaiming the planet and establishing himself as the new ruler of the empire.[14]

The harsh desert landscapes and the adventures that await for travelers in them have fascinated Miyazaki since reading Fukushima's *Devil of the Desert* and drawing his own manga *People of the Desert*, and it can be speculated that Herbert's novel held the same appeal for him. It is also easy to spot the many superficial similarities between the two works: Nausicaa's status as a leader who deeply inspires her followers, eventually as a messianic figure, is strongly reminiscent of Paul's. The wise old woman of the valley of the wind, and to a certain extant Nausicaa herself, are also similar to the matriarchal society of Bene Gesserit and their leading "Reverend Mothers" (including Paul's mother Jessica) in their great knowledge, wisdom, and strong mental abilities, although Miyazaki clearly viewed the influence of such strong female figures on the ongoing history of the world he created in a positive manner while Herbert was at best ambivalent about it. Both characters of Gurney Halleck and Duncan Idaho, warriors-supreme in the service of House Atreides, are strongly reminiscent of Master Yupa in Miyazaki's manga.[15]

The influence of Herbert's novel on Miyazaki's manga goes much deeper than these similarities. Herbert was inspired to write his novel while working on a magazine article dealing with the struggle of the United State's Department of Agriculture with the spreading of desert sands, and not unlike Miyazaki's awed reaction to the story about the survivability of wildlife under harsh conditions, Herbert was also impressed by the sheer power of nature and environment to overcome even the greatest achievements of men, noting in his article proposal how the great cities of the past have drowned under the sand.[16] At its core, *Dune* is the story of people who learn to adapt to the ruthless environmental conditions of the desert planet, the Fremen among whom Paul finds refuge, and whose assimilation into this environment allows them to use its natural resources (as the giant sandworms they ride—another inspiration for the giant Ohmu in the manga, according to Miyazaki[17]) to their ends. The desert world of Herbert's novel is a deadly place, yet it holds its own undeniable beauty. The same is very true for the post-apocalyptic world of Miyazaki's manga—the Sea of Decay may be highly toxic, but living creatures exist and evolve within it. Like the Fremen in Herbert's novel, the Sea of Decay also hosts two communities of human beings: the Wormhandlers who take advantage of their ability to survive within the toxic environment to provide different services for the other human communities (and in the course of the story become Nausicaa's most devoted followers) and the Forest People, who are even more deeply assimilated into the Sea of Decay's ecological system and with whom Nausicaa shares a deep mental connection. Both communities represent the ideal destiny that Nausicaa has in mind for the human race: not overcoming the harsh environment that surrounds it but learning to fit within it, recognizing that, not unlike Herbert's desert planet, it has its own beauty.

The need to assimilate into and keep evolving within the deadly environment is taken to its greatest extreme in the conclusion of both works. In Herbert's novel, Paul threatens to destroy the desert planet's entire supply of spice and bring the whole human race into oblivion if he is not made ruler of not only Arrakis but the entire universe. In doing so, he forces the universe to abandon its old regime and accept the hegemony of the unforgiving desert world and its people. In Miyazaki's manga, Nausicaa actually goes a step further: in the concluding chapters of the manga, she learns that her world is being manipulated by the collective consciousness of scientists from the pre-apocalyptic era, who plan to eventually restore the world to its previous state after cleansing it. Nausicaa put an end to this plan, by destroying the crypt in which these scientists reside and enforcing the hegemony of the people of her world—who struggle to survive—and their right to evolve as they see fit. Such a vote of confidence in humanity is inspiring but also chilling, given the cruelty humanity is capable of as seen throughout the series. Yet the concluding panels imply that Nausicaa has fulfilled her mission of teaching the people of her world the value of peace.

Douglas Trumbull's 1972 film *Silent Running* is another example of an environmentally aware work of science fiction that appears to have inspired Miyazaki's manga. Unlike the highly detailed worlds presented in both Aldiss' and Herbert's novels, Trumbull's film is a more low-key affair, confined to a small environment—a spaceship preserving the final samples of trees and plants in greenhouse-like structures, after all the flora has disappeared from Earth. When orders arrive to destroy the greenhouses and return to Earth, crewman Freeman Lowell (Bruce Dern) who made the greenhouses his life's work, murders his fellow crewmembers and escapes with the ship deep into space.

Though it failed to make a big impression at the box office upon its initial release—the film plays more like a meditative drama about guilt and loneliness rather than the space-adventure that its audience was probably expecting—*Silent Running* has gained significant following and acclaim in the years that followed. The film's portrayal of cute, small robots has also inspired the beloved R2D2 character from George Lucas' *Star Wars* (1977),[18] and its convincing design of a futuristic environment that combines the look of used and home-modified technology with colorful natural landscape has been imitated in many subsequent productions, such as Pixar's *Wall-E* (2008).

The film's environmental theme and its portrayal of a struggle to preserve the natural environment show a strong influence on *Nausicaa of the Valley of the Wind*. Like the protagonist of Trumbull's film who takes care of the last remaining trees and plants in his greenhouses, Nausicaa keeps her own lab in which she manages to grow non-polluted flora. Both characters believe that they bring hope to the world, but the world is not interested in this kind of salvation: Lowell's other crew members, who have grown used to eating synthetic food and living in a sterile world with no plants, believe that their mission of caring for the greenhouses is a waste of time, just as the kingdoms that surround the Valley of the Wind prefer to go to war over domination of the world rather than its restoration. The question of how far the struggle for the restoration of the world can go is also a key theme in both *Silent Running* and Miyazaki's manga: Lowell chooses violence, killing his crewmates and also himself, leaving the greenhouses he cared for to flourish without a human presence; Nausicaa chooses life, destroying her lab and going on a quest to save humanity, believing that it will eventually save the world.

Miyazaki's manga drew additional inspiration from other science fiction works that were not necessarily environmentally themed. One such major source was probably *Uchū Senkan Yamato* (*Space Cruiser*

Yamato or *Star Blazers* as it was known in its English dub) a 1974 grand-scale animated space-opera television series. The show told the heroic story of a team of astronauts onboard a World War II warship retooled for space-travel, who go on a quest to find the distant planet Iscandar, which possesses a technology capable of cleansing the Earth of deadly radiation pollution caused by an alien race's nuclear attacks.

While not an instant success upon its initial broadcast, *Star Blazers* managed to gather a steadily growing fanbase, and expanded into a franchise of more television shows and films.[19] A notable element in each new production of the franchise was the apocalyptic threat to Earth vividly portrayed in scenes of mass-destruction, corresponding with the fears that have accompanied Japan since the end of the war—from the atomic bomb, through natural disasters, to the oil shocks of the 1970s that threatened to bring Japan to financial ruin. Though the militaristic response to such a threat presented by the franchise was far from Miyazaki's ideological worldview, there is more than a passing resemblance between the apocalyptic scenes of *Star Blazers* and those seen at the opening of each episode of *Future Boy Conan*, notably in the portrayal of strange aircraft looming over a modern landscape of tall urban buildings, followed by scenes of destruction of the modern civilization.

Star Blazers shows a deeper and more significant influence on *Nausicaa of the Valley of the Wind* in its depiction of the forbidden paradise. Like planet Iscandar on the franchise's first television show, the storyline of almost each subsequent production featured a seemingly perfect, technologically advanced world of natural beauty, which upon closer inspection is revealed to be nothing more than a giant cemetery— with almost all its residents perished in some kind of disaster, and its only remaining survivor (a female character whose message to Earth usually sends the Yamato crew on its long journey) left to mourn at the ruins of her people's once-great civilization.

This forbidden paradise holds a great temptation—indeed, in the first television show of the *Star Blazers* franchise, several crewmembers of the Yamato declare mutiny and announce their intent to stay on the planet—which is very similar to the temptation that Nausicaa faces toward the end of her journey. Upon arriving at a beautiful garden, well attended and containing clean and breathable air, Nausicaa is offered and even pressured by the mysterious "Master" into abandoning her journey and staying at the place. The garden is not unlike the seemingly utopian dead worlds of the *Star Blazers* franchise or, for that matter, like Nausicaa's smaller-scale lab: an experiment in developing a beautiful and clean environment, devoid of the pollution and wars that plague the outside world, but also of the element that led to these problems—human presence. Even the temptation of living in a paradise and being comforted by false memories of the loving mother she never had is not enough to make Nausicaa give up on humanity, and she chooses to leave the garden. Unlike the female rulers of the dead worlds of *Star Blazers*, Nausicaa does not hang onto death but to life; her salvation of the human race comes not through magical technology but through teaching.

Another science fiction work that had a strong influence on the visual portrayal of the apocalyptic world of Miyazaki's manga is the comic series *Arzach* by French artist Jean Giraud, originally published in 1975 under the pseudonym Moebius, used by Giraud for most of his science fiction works. The series consisted of four silent stories told through pictures alone with no text, each following a square-jawed warrior who rides a pre-historical flying beast and gets mixed up in weird adventures.

Miyazaki met Giraud while he was working on *Nausicaa of the Valley of the Wind*, and the two artists became friends; Giraud spoke highly of Miyazaki's work, and the two shared a joint exhibition of works in France in 2005. Miyazaki claimed that, while he appreciated *Arzach*, by the time he began working on the manga his own style had solidified enough that Giraud's comics had only a minor influence on him, if any.[20] Yet a comparison between the two works makes this influence undeniable.

Arzach was published in the comic magazine *Metal Hurlant*. Co-founded by Giraud himself, the magazine was a revolutionary publication that featured adult-oriented science fiction and fantasy stories which launched the careers of many leading artists, and contributed greatly to the recognition of comics as a form of sophisticated art—*Arzach* has been praised for unique visual storytelling.[21] Like Corben's *Rowlf*, though to a lesser extent, certain elements of *Arzach* feel needlessly exploitive (not one but two stories in the series begin with the protagonist peeping on a naked woman), although the surreal, loosely plotted atmosphere of the series provides it something of a context—as explained by Giraud himself in the introduction to the American collected edition of the series,[22] it was meant to reflect subconscious mindsets, forbidden pleasures, and fears that influenced its design of alien worlds.

While this theme did not find its way to Miyazaki's manga, other elements from Giraud's series, especially visual ones, did. Panels showing Nausicaa riding her steam-powered glider are strongly similar to panels showing Giraud's protagonist riding on his flying beast. The second *Arzach* story features not only a deadly flora environment but also a monstrous beast very similar to the god-warrior from *Nausicaa of the Valley of the Wind*. And like Miyazaki's manga, Giraud's series is rife with ancient abandoned structures, the remains of a long-gone civilization.

Arzach also influenced *Nausicaa of the Valley of the Wind* in its aesthetic approach. While the silent pages of Corben's *Rowlf* influenced Miyazaki's handling of action scenes, the silent pages of *Arzach* had a more atmospheric influence. Three out of the four *Arzach* stories begin with the protagonist approaching a weird-looking, alien environment that he's ready to explore, and as he explores it the story's visuals emphasize how the place's surroundings and inhabitants dwarf him. Miyazaki's manga begins in a similar manner, with Nausicaa silently riding her glider into a cave filled with strange but deadly plants, finding a complete Ohmu shell. Like Giruad, Miyazaki has used silent pages to make his readers both feel awe of the strange world that he created, and at the same time appreciate it for its beauty.

While Giraud and his colleagues at *Metal Hurlant* were busy revolutionizing adult-oriented science fiction storytelling in comics, another French artist was busy doing the same in animation, and also ended up influencing Miyazaki's epic. In 1973, filmmaker Rene Laloux gained worldwide acclaim for his cutout feature *La Planete sauvage* (literally "The Savage Planet," released in English-speaking countries under the title *Fantastic Planet*), the first in a short but influential series of animated science fiction films.[23] Though Miyazaki claimed to be unimpressed with *Fantastic Planet* upon seeing it (he acknowledged that the design of the world in which the film takes place was imaginative, but argued that the plot was too thin[24]), its influence on his manga— visually and thematically—is obvious.

Based on a novel by Pierre Pairault (who wrote under the pseudonym Stefan Wul), *Fantastic Planet* takes place on Ygam, a world populated by the Draags—a race of giant, bald, blue-skinned, and red-eyed creatures. The Draags are a technologically advanced culture, and many of them keep members of a primitive race—human beings known as "Oms"—as their pets. The film's protagonist is Terr, an Om child who is taken as a pet by a Draag girl, manages to educate himself, joins a tribe of free Oms, and helps them in their struggle for survival.

Like Grimault, Laloux has also experienced the horrors of the Nazi occupation in France, as did his artistic collaborator on the production of *Fantastic Planet*, cartoonist Roland Topor. The struggle against tyranny is a major theme in the film and in Laloux's subsequent works, though the anarchistic and occasionally violent approach to this struggle practiced by the protagonists of Grimault's *The Shepherdess and the Chimneysweep* was rejected in Laloux's film in favor of a more intellectual approach: it is first and foremost the self-education of the oppressed population that sets it on its path to freedom. Moreover, the final resolution of the conflict between the humans and the Draag comes not from a military victory but rather from the realization that each population needs the other, and peace must be achieved—not unlike the approach that Nausicaa preaches throughout the manga.

The influence of other elements from Laloux's film can be seen in *Nausicaa of the Valley of the Wind*. The name "Oms," given to members of the human race in *Fantastic Planet*, may have been one of the sources of inspiration for the name of the giant worm-like dwellers of Miyazaki's manga. Like the Sea of Decay, the wild environment that Terr escapes to in Laloux's film is filled with deadly mutated forms of flora and fauna that humans often view in awe and helplessness. One particular visual resemblance between the two works comes from a chilling scene in *Fantastic Planet*, in which the Draag come to exterminate human presence in the wild using chemical warfare. The design of the Draag characters in this scene—wearing gasmasks and leading hounds—is almost identical to that of the Wormhandlers in *Nausicaa of the Valley of the Wind*. Miyazaki appears to have reversed the roles in this scene in his manga, where the Wormhandlers are actually the population assimilated into the natural environment (like the humans in Laloux's film) rather than those who come to destroy it.

Laloux's was not the only filmmaker who attempted to produce adult-oriented animated features with post-apocalyptic themes in the 1970s and early 1980s. American directors also experimented in the genre, though with far less success and certainly less artistic ambition. A prime example is *Wizards*, directed by animator Ralph Bakshi, which opened in 1977. The film takes place in a world devastated by nuclear war, in which the population is divided into beautiful fairy-like creatures who master the art of magic, and ugly mutants who use military war technology. A war breaks out between the two groups when Blackwolf, the evil leader of the mutants, discovers the ultimate weapon to inspire his troops and scare his enemies—propaganda footage from Nazi Germany.

Prior to directing *Wizards*, Bakshi was known mostly for animated films about urban life in America of the 1970s, featuring risqué humor and often strong erotic content.[25] These films have both admirers and detractors, but as Bakshi's first foray into fantasy filmmaking, *Wizards* features almost all the elements that gave the director a bad name with few redeeming qualities. It is shamelessly exploitive in both its design of female characters (emphasizing their big breasts through skimpy clothing) and scenes of genocide warfare (despite the parallelization that the film makes between Nazi Germany and the mutant army, it in fact adopts a very unpleasant Nazi-like aesthetic in presenting the good fairies as beautiful and noble and the evil mutants as hideously ugly and deformed). The film's story is a complete mess that moves clumsily between unfunny slapstick humor and bad attempts at serious drama.

Yet despite being an artistic failure, *Wizards* was a commercial success, a fact even referred to by Miyazaki in his proposal to adapt *Rowlf* into an animated feature. Minor elements in Bakshi's film appear to have influenced Miyazaki while working on *Nausicaa of the Valley of the Wind*: the silent, devastated post-war landscapes that the heroes pass through in the course of Bakshi's film, presented in a dark color palate, certainly recall similar landscapes in Miyazaki's manga. The character of Avatar, the wizard leader of the fairies, may have contributed somewhat to the design of bearded characters of the Valley of the Wind. The most notable visual idea borrowed from Bakshi by Miyazaki is having two-legged animals as riding mounts—though in *Wizards* this idea seems to be just another prop thrown in, while in *Nausicaa of the Valley of the Wind* it feels like an integral part of the world's ecosystem.

The success of *Wizards* inspired other American animated post-apocalyptic productions, and one such high-profile production was *Heavy Metal* (1981), inspired by and adapting several stories from the *Metal Hurlant* magazine, founded by Giraud (the name *Heavy Metal* is the title of the magazine's American edition). As in *Wizards*, *Heavy Metal* is a shamelessly exploitive work that cannot quite find its own voice and decide if it is played for laughs or a serious drama. It does, however, feature slicker design and animation than Bakshi's film, as well as a far more entertaining script. A brief scene in one particular segment of the film, *Den* (adapted from a story by Richard Corben) may have provided Miyazaki with some inspiration for *Nausicaa of the Valley of the Wind*, as it features giant insects flying over an exotic fantasy-world. An even stronger influence may have come from *Taarna*, the film's final segment, which follows a female warrior on her way to destroy a giant glowing green orb that has turned a group of peaceful people into bloodthirsty monsters.

Taarna was originally planned as an adaptation of Giraud's *Arzach*, but legal complications prevented the film's producers from acquiring the rights.[26] The segment produced for the film borrows the concept of a protagonist who travels through a post-apocalyptic world in on a flying creature from Giraud's comics, replacing the male protagonist with a female heroine and abandoning the abstract narrative in favor of a more standard good-versus-evil story.

Though *Taarna* bears the same unpleasant feeling of an adolescent fantasy that accompanies the rest of the film (one scene features completely needless nudity of the protagonist, who for the rest of the film wears a fetish outfit) and falls into the same ideological pit as *Wizards* in its simplistic presentation of good-looking people fighting ugly deformed enemies, it is a well-told and well-animated story, significantly better than other segments in the film. Certain elements in it, as noted before, may have inspired Miyazaki's manga: the idea of recasting *Arzach* with a fierce female warrior, the flying beast that the heroine rides on (and in *Heavy Metal* this beast moves somewhat mechanically, resembling not only Nausicaa's glider but also the small Torumekian fighter-planes), the strong emotional bond she shares with the beast she rides (which is not unlike Nausicaa's bond with animals—in particular the two-legged mounts of her world), and the heroine's quest to save the world from an apocalyptic disaster, which takes her to a small seedy bar in a remote town (an obvious reference to westerns, but also recalling the small populated towns that Miyazaki's manga occasionally takes its protagonists to). The heroine's final stand, in which she puts an end to the glowing orb, also echoes the ending of *Nausicaa of the Valley of the Wind*, in which Nausicaa puts an end to everything that may link her people to the "old world."

Even considering *Taarna* as a sufficiently entertaining piece, it was— not unlike the rest of *Heavy Metal* or *Wizards* before it—little more than a juvenile affair, lacking any real depth, claiming to be "adult" due to its portrayals of sex and violence. The influence Miyazaki may have drawn from it demonstrates less respect to it and more an ambition to show how a serious, post-apocalyptic drawn story can be done right.

The Blue-Clad Messiah

There are two versions regarding the circumstances that led to Miyazaki's invitation to draw *Nausicaa of the Valley of the Wind* for Animage: one claims that Miyazaki proposed the project as an animated film but publisher Tokuma was hesitant about funding a feature that was not based on a popular manga, so he drew the comics to prepare the commercial ground for a possible adaptation; another version claims

The optimistic ending of the film version of *Nausicaa of the Valley of the Wind*, in which the devastated world's population accepts the heroine as their messiah and there is hope for mankind, is contrasted by the ending of the manga version—the heroine is still accepted as a messiah, but one with a very different gospel.

that Miyazaki drew the manga before being offered the opportunity to adapt it to film.[27] Either way, the manga has proven to be highly popular among the magazine's readers, and in 1983 Miyazaki took his first break from drawing it in order to work on an animated feature adaptation of the manga, released the following year.

Nausicaa of the Valley of the Wind was the second feature directed by Miyazaki, and the first based on a protagonist created by him (though, as noted in the previous chapter, his approach to Lupin in *The Castle of Cagliostro* was a rather radical interpretation of the character). The film's production involved several of Miyazaki's veteran colleagues (notably Isao Takahata, who served as one of the producers, and Yōichi Kotabe who worked on the film as an animator), but it also brought together a new core workforce that would accompany Miyazaki's features for many years to come. The most prominent example is young composer Hisaishi Joe, whose score for the film combines different styles (symphonic, electronic, and even a children's lullaby) into a single, beautiful, musical vision. Another example is the team of animators working for the studio recruited for the film's production, Topcraft.

The people of Topcraft played an important role in the development of Japan's post-war animation industry. As early as the 1960s, American producers Jules Bass and Arthur Rankin have outsourced animation jobs to Japan, beginning with American stop-motion productions such as *Rudolph the Red-Nosed Reindeer* (1964), moving on to cel-animated productions, employing different animation studios as Tōei and Tezuka's Mushi production. By the 1970s, the animators employed by Bass and Rankin had founded Topcraft, working with the two American producers on grandiose adaptations of classic fantasy novels such as J.R.R. Tolkien's *The Hobbit* (1977) and Peter S. Beagle's *The Last Unicorn* (1982). Though sub-contracting of animation works to Japan and other Asian countries remains a commonplace practice to this day, Rankin, Bass, and the Topcraft animators were pioneers in the field, and by the time the studio worked on *Nausicaa of the Valley of the Wind* its animators were renowned for the high quality of their work; during the film's production the studio had also assigned some of its top animators to work on even the lowliest jobs, giving it a feeling of unparalleled attention to detail.[28]

Though produced while Miyazaki's manga was still in its early chapters, the story of the manga was already too complex and too far from completion to fit within the film's two-hour runtime. This meant that, in adapting the source material, Miyazaki had to trim the original storyline considerably. In the film, the Dorok Empire is never seen or mentioned, and the plot focuses on the conflict between Torumekia and Pejite. The crash-landing of the Pejite plane in the Valley of the Wind is a significant event in the film, as it is in the manga, but it leads to the arrival of Kushana and her troops to the Valley as conquerors rather than military allies. The true struggle in the film is not between armies, but between mankind and nature.

As noted above, it would have been impossible to bring the entire storyline of the then-incomplete manga into a single film. However, other than changing key elements in the plot, the film also simplifies it considerably, especially when it comes to its two main female characters and their motivations. Kushana, in the film, is reduced to a one-dimensional villain: instead of the ambitious military leader whose hard life made her a hard person, in the film she is driven by revenge alone and the constant destruction of nature becomes something of a twisted ideology for her, having lost an arm in a struggle with one of the Sea of Decay's creatures. The film emphasizes Kushana's detachment from humanity and the living world—she is part-machine (using a mechanical arm instead of the arm she lost, an idea that may have been borrowed from *Heavy Metal*), lacking any kind of emotion other than hatred of the world that surrounds her and other people in it, whereas in the manga she was every bit as human as Nausicaa. The only meaningful (and very

short) relationship that Kushana manages to establish in the film is with
the God Warrior, which she resurrects and sees as an extension of herself
and her ambitions, a device of total destruction. This resembles an
element that will appear toward the end of the manga (years after the
production of the film)—like Nausicaa in the concluding chapters of the
manga, the film's Kushana becomes a mother to the God Warrior, and
like Nausicaa she eventually fails to keep it alive. But in the manga, even
the God Warrior managed to transcend its monstrous nature and
(inspired by Nausicaa) become a compassionate creature. In the film, it
is reduced to a mere plot-device, a mindless monster.

Nausicaa herself is also a radically simplified version of the manga's
protagonist. In the manga, Nausicaa is on a constant search for answers
to the problems of her world while in the film she already has all the
answers. She knows better than everyone what needs to be done and is
utterly compassionate and forgiving (a key scene in the film has
Torumekian troops killing King Jhil; other than a brief moment of anger,
Nausicaa never shows any kind of resentment toward Kushana for
killing her father and the subject is in fact never touched upon
throughout the rest of the film). Though arguments can be made against
Napier's observation of Nausicaa being a "boring" character in the
manga, it is certainly true in the film: she is, as Napier described, too
perfect to be a believable person.

Yet for a character whose main role is to be right all the time, Nausicaa
remains strangely ineffectual throughout the course of the film. She
preaches, but almost nobody listens. Unlike the charismatic protagonist
of the manga, who managed to make people follow her path even when
she wasn't sure just what this path was, in the film she almost never
manages to convert people from their violent way of life to her pacifism.
Kushana remains a militant figure all throughout, the people of the
Valley look up to their princess but respond in violence toward the
Torumekians once they suspect she was killed, and the only exception is
Asbel, who eventually sees the wisdom of Nausicaa's worldview (but the
film also implies that he is attracted to Nausicaa, so his conversion to her
belief is hardly a pure ideological matter; in fact, the film even implies
that this attraction is mutual, in sharp contrast to Nausicaa's asexuality
in the manga).

What does make Nausicaa save the world at the end of the film is a
miracle—and one that she has no control over. After apparently dying in
a horrible manner while trying to stop a raging heard of creatures from
the sea of decay, Nausicaa is resurrected by the same creatures,

immediately prompting all warring parties around her to accept her as the blue-clad messiah who preaches the truth. This ending, a sharp contrast to the manga in which Nausicaa played a very active role in saving humanity (and did so in a very non-messianic manner, insisting that the human race will determine its own path rather than the one set for it) makes Nausicaa an even less complex character than she was before in turning her into a character that has a pre-determined destiny to save the world through heroic deeds (her apparent self-sacrifice is possibly another reference to the character of Taarna from *Heavy Metal*).

Despite the film's shortcomings, it remains a well-told and gorgeous-looking work. The story keeps a brisk pace without giving up on its source material's rich world-building through beautifully detailed backgrounds of the Valley of the Wind and the Sea of Decay. This sense of worldbuilding benefits greatly from the coloring work, giving a new dimension to the manga's original black-and-white drawings: the Valley of the Wind can now be appreciated for its brightly colored beauty as a small rural community whose people live off the land (not unlike High Harbor from *Future Boy Conan* or the rural communities of *Heidi, Girl of the Alps* and *Anne of Green Gables*). The Sea of Decay, colored in different shades of green and full of spores that fill the air, delivers a true presence of something non-human that slowly takes over. Characters gain an extra dimension through coloring as well: Nausicaa's is an expressive character whose both vigorous mood and compassionate nature are emphasized through the red hair that frames her face; Kushana, the Norse-looking princess, is even closer in her design in the film to the Snow Queen from Atamanov's film thanks to careful color-coding of her white outfit combined with grey metallic armor-pieces that deliver a feeling of cold aristocracy.

Nausicaa of the Valley of the Wind served as an interesting lesson for Miyazaki about the limitations that accompany a two-hour film, and how it cannot match the epic scope of a manga that eventually ran over a thousand pages. He quickly put this lesson to good use, however, when he produced his following epics.

Notes

1   McCarthy, Hayao Miyazaki, *Master of Japanese Animation*, 40–41.
2   For a discussion of the series, see Daniel Thomas, "People of the Desert (Sabaku no Tami)—Hayao Miyazaki's 1969 Manga," *Ghibli Blog* (2014).

Available online: http://ghiblicon.blogspot.co.il/2011/04/miyazakis-first-manga-people-of-desert.html

3	Alexander Key, *The Incredible Tide* (New York: Open Road, 2014).

4	For example, Robert Moore has noted in the introduction to the essays anthology *Joss Whedon: The Complete Companion* the film version of *Nausicaa of the Valley of the Wind* as one of the few examples for popular works "with girl heroes" (London, Titan Books, 2012), 19–21.

5	Arthur Waley, "The Lady who Loved Insects." In *Anthology of Japanese Literature, from the Earliest Era to the Mid-Nineteenth Century*, ed. Donald Keene (New York: Grove Press, 1955), 170–176.

6	Bernard Evslin, *Gods, Demigods and Demons: An Encyclopedia of Greek Mythology* (New York: Scholastic Book Services, 1975), 145–147.

7	Susan Napier, "Vampires, Psychic Girls, Flying Women and Sailor Scouts: Four faces of the young female in Japanese Popular Culture." In *The Worlds of Japanese Popular Culture*, ed. Dolores P. Martinez (Cambridge: Cambridge University Press, 1998), 91–109.

8	Miyazaki, *Starting Point*, 249–251.

9	Richard Corben, *Rowlf/Underground 3* (New York: Catalan Communications, 1987), 17–48.

10	Hayao Miyazaki, *The Art of Nausicaa of the Valley of the Wind, Watercolor Impressions* (San Francisco: Viz Media, 2007), 147–148; 176–184.

11	Robert Herman, *This Borrowed Earth: Lessons from the Fifteen Worst Environmental Disasters Around the World* (New York: Palgrave Macmillan, 2010), 9–31.

12	McCarthy, *Hayao Miyazaki, Master of Japanese Animation*, 74–75.

13	Brian Aldiss, *Hothouse* (London: Penguin Classics, 2008). According to McCarthy (*Hayao Miyazaki, Master of Japanese Animation*, 75), Miyazaki was impressed with the novel's depiction of plant life, but less with the development of its human characters.

14	Frank Herbert, *Dune* (New York: Ace Books, 2010).

15	Interestingly, British actor Patrick Stewart, who played Gurney Halleck in David Lynch's 1984 film version of *Dune*, also voiced Master Yupa's character in the 2005 English dub of the film version of *Nausicaa of the Valley of the Wind*.

16	Brian Herbert and Kevin J. Anderson, *The Road to Dune* (New York: Tor Books, 2005), 263–268.

17	Miyazaki, *Starting Point*, 416.

18	See Kristen Brennan, "The Droids," *Star Wars Origins* (2006). Available online: http://moongadget.com/origins/droids.html

19	For more details about the franchise and its impact on the Japanese animation industry and its fandom, this author strongly recommends Tim Eldred's 2005 documentary film *Space Battleship Yamato: The Making of an Anime Legend*.

20 "A Talk between Hayao Miyazaki and Moebius," *Nausicaa.net* (2005). Available online: http://www.nausicaa.net/miyazaki/interviews/miyazaki_moebious.html

21 Matthew Screech, "Moebius Nouveau Realism and Science Fiction" in *The Francophone Bande Dessinne*, eds. Charles Forsdick, Laurence Grove and Libbie McQuillan (New York: Rodopi, 2005), 97–114.

22 Jean Giarud, *Moebius 2: Arzach and Other Fantasy Stories* (New York: The Marvel Entertainment Group, 1987).

23 Raz Greenberg, "The Illustrated Man," *Salon Futura* (2011). Available online: http://www.salonfutura.net/2011/02/the-illustrated-man/

24 Miyazaki, *Starting Point*, 120–122.

25 Grant, *Masters of Animation*, 18–29.

26 "Creation of the Taarna Sequence," *Celebrating Taarna* (2002). Available online: http://www.taarna.net/history.html

27 Erin Finnegan, "Shelf Life: Culture Club" (2011). Available online: http://www.animenewsnetwork.com/shelf-life/2011-04-04

28 Clements, *Anime: A History*, 106–109, 180.

Chapter 5

BRINGING IT ALL TOGETHER: STUDIO GHIBLI

Several months after the *Nausicaa of the Valley of the Wind* manga started its run in 1982, Miyazaki was hired, along with his colleagues Isao Takahata, Yasuo Ōtsuka, and Yoshifumi Kondō, to take part in the production of *Little Nemo: Adventures in Slumberland*. The ambitious American/Japanese coproduction adapted the classic comic strip by cartoonist and animation pioneer Winsor McCay about a boy who, each night, goes on a strange adventure in his dreams. McCay's work had many fans on both sides of the Pacific: in fact, the project was initiated by Japanese producer Yutaka Fujioka, the president of Tokyo Movie Shinsha, the studio that previously employed Miyazaki and Takahata on *Moomins*, the *Panda! Go Panda!* films, and the *Lupin* productions. Many other notable figures have been involved with different stages of the production including Jean Giraud, renowned science fiction author Ray Bradbury, and screenwriter Chris Columbus (future director of the early *Harry Potter* films).

Unfortunately, *Little Nemo: Adventures in Slumberland* proved to be a highly problematic production, stretching across almost a decade before the film's eventual release in 1989 to a box office failure. Miyazaki and Takahata left the production only a few months after being invited to work on the film due to creative differences (Miyazaki did not like the idea of a fantasy world that exists purely as a dream; Takahata's proposal for a story that tells how the protagonist grows up was rejected).[1] Yoshifumi Kondō remained with the production until 1985, and directed a short pilot-film meant to demonstrate the project's concept. This pilot shows the huge influence that Miyazaki had on Kondō—it is essentially a breathtaking six-minute flight sequence in which the protagonist rides his flying bed, accompanied by another boy who flies an ancient plane drawn in loving detail—and it set up the general mood and style for the film as it was eventually released four years later (despite its troubled production, it should be noted that *Little Nemo: Adventures in Slumberland* is actually a well-animated and highly entertaining film, if not a very deep one). Kondō himself, however, also left the production shortly after completing the pilot.[2]

Even though Miyazaki's involvement with *Little Nemo: Adventures in Slumberland* was short, his time in the United States was well spent. He attended a lecture by legendary Disney animators Frank Thomas and Ollie Johnston (both also involved with the production of the film) and it was probably during this period that he was exposed to another important artistic influence on his feature films—the work of Canadian animator Frederic Back (1924–2013).[3]

A French immigrant to Canada, Back was a gifted painter who turned to film and television production in the 1950s, working on everything from film opening titles to animation. In 1980, he received his first Academy Award nomination for his animated short *All Nothing*, an amusing and environmentally aware version of the biblical creation story. Back's next three films made prior to his retirement had similar emphasis on environmental issues: *Crac!*, which won him an Academy Award in 1982, followed the industrial development of Canada through the story of a rocking chair and a rural community; *The Man Who Planted Trees*, which won him his second Academy Award, adapted the classic story by French writer Jean Giono about a shepherd who heals the wounds of a ravaged French county through the simple act of planting a forest; and finally *The Mighty River*, nominated for an Academy Award in 1994, a cautionary tale about the history of the St. Lawrence River in Quebec.

Miyazaki was highly impressed upon seeing *Crac!* for the first time. He was captivated by the lively way in which Back drew and animated natural scenery and plants; indeed, the film features beautifully drawn painterly backgrounds of the Quebec forests and rivers, whose beauty does not come from their wild, untamed nature—it comes from the harmonious way of life adopted by the people who live among them, people who have learned to co-exist with nature. *Crac!* opens with a tree being cut and used to build a chair by a local farmer, who later sows and harvests fields of hay. This kind of ideal living off the land involves just the right amount of interference with nature while allowing it to thrive. But when such interference goes beyond the necessary needs of man— when the natural forests and even the fields sowed by man must make way for railroads, roads, and power-plants, as seen in the film—mankind loses something. Human imagination is hurt as well: while the children of the film's protagonist are seen throughout it playing with their father's rocking chair, turning it in their imagination into a vessel that takes them on grand adventures, in the modern era this chair finds itself in a museum surrounded by soulless modern paintings. In the film's final amusing twist, children who come to the museum find the chair far more interesting than the paintings that surround it.

The Man Who Planted Trees also shows how interference with nature can have positive consequences. The film portrays a man-made forest as something that improves the quality of life—not just environmentally but also politically, a strong symbol of peace that even the horrors of war cannot defy (the film tells of how minor wood chopping took place in the forest during the war, but its relative distance made such actions non-profitable and they were quickly abandoned). The fact that this forest is man-made is lost on pretty much everyone—including the authorities, who place the forest under protection, believing it to be a natural phenomenon—besides the film's narrator who knows the truth. The importance of such man-made initiatives is made very clear in the film, and Miyazaki wrote of it enthusiastically in his review of it. Miyazaki was not the only person captivated by the shepherd's character in the film: long before Back directed his adaptation, readers who fell in love with the character wondered whether it was a true story and if they could visit the beautiful forest described in the book. Giono must have been heartbroken to disappoint his readers and tell them that the story was entirely fictional.

The first signs of the influence that Back's films had on Miyazaki are evident in *Nausicaa of the Valley of the Wind*: as noted in the previous chapter, the portrayal of the Valley of the Wind as a community that lives off the land and respects nature is highly positive, not unlike the community portrayed at *Crac!*. The manga's concluding chapters also reveal how man-made forests can change human life in a manner that echoes *The Man Who Planted Trees* (although the manga is far more ambivalent on whether this change is positive or negative). The influence of Back's films, however, is much stronger on Miyazaki's later works directed in his own studio.

Old and New

The animated adaptation of *Nausicaa of the Valley of the Wind* performed adequately at the Japanese box-office, and found even greater success on the newly introduced home-viewing platforms of the early 1980s, VHS and Laserdisc. This led to a decision by Tokuma Shoten (publisher of the *Animage* magazine) to invest in the foundation of an animation studio headed by Miyazaki and Takahata. The name Ghibli (pronounced ji-bu-ri) was chosen for the new studio by Miyazaki himself, after a famous aircraft model designed by the legendary Italian engineer Giovanni Caproni, showcasing Miyazaki's love for aircraft and flying. Recruiting its initial workforce from both old colleagues as well as Topcraft animators who participated in the production of *Nausicaa of the Valley of the Wind*, the studio began working on its first project—Miyazaki's third feature-length film, *Castle in the Sky* (*Tenkū no Shiro Rapyuta*).

Taking place in a fictional rural country that strongly resembles late nineteenth-century England, the film follows two orphaned children— Pazu, a young miner from a small town, and Sheeta, a mysterious girl who literally fell from the sky, and their quest to discover the legendary flying island Laputa. The island plays an important role in the heritage of both protagonists; Pazu's father was obsessed with its discovery, something that made him an object of mockery, while Sheeta is a descendant of the royal family that ruled the island before coming to live among the people of the Earth. Other, more sinister, parties are also looking for the flying island; the government wishes to get its hands on its legendary treasures and incredible powers, assigning ruthless agent Muska (who is also a descendant of the Island's royal family) and a battalion of army soldiers to the task. Aided by a gang of air-pirates, Pazu and Sheeta must not only find Laputa, but also make sure that its secrets do not fall into the wrong hands.

As in *Nausicaa of the Valley of the Wind*, *Castle in the Sky* was partially inspired by real world events. During a research trip to Wales in 1984, when production was already underway and the initial plot had been sketched, Miyazaki had witnessed the struggle of the miners against the British government's decision to shut down the coal mines. Other than appealing to his leftist political sensibilities, this struggle also represented to Miyazaki the struggle between two different styles of life: that of the hard-working people who live off the land, develop their own machines and technology and make wise use of it; and that of those in power, whose mass-produced industrial technology is used for oppression. The sight of abandoned mines, filled with equipment left unused, was seen by Miyazaki as an attack on not only the miners' means of living, but also their way of life.[4] The passage from the traditional, self-sustaining rural community to the modern industrial society, presented as tragic but unavoidable in Back's *Crac!* is shown vividly in *Castle in the Sky*—even before government representatives come to cause trouble, the hardships of the mining community are evident everywhere, from the diminishing production of the mines through the ancient homes of community members that have seen better days, to the fields that slowly make way (again, as in Back's film) to roads and railroads.

Castle in the Sky is also deeply rooted within Miyazaki's filmography of the two decades that preceded it. At times it feels like the film that Miyazaki never got to direct at Tōei; other times it brings to mind the rural European landscapes seen in the *Calpis/World Masterpiece Theatre* shows and the chase scenes of the *Lupin III* television series and *The Castle of Cagliostro*; the epic scope of *Future Boy Conan* also echoes strongly in the film. The works of filmmakers, animators, and authors who influenced Miyazaki are also referenced throughout the film. *Castle in the Sky* may have been Miyazaki's third feature-film, but it was the first film in which he managed to bring together his past experience and influences into a single, coherent, original vision.

The film's two protagonists are the strongest evidence of this solidified vision. Pazu is, like many male protagonists in Miyazaki's previous works from Ken to Conan, the civilized boy: he grew up in the small community that lives off the land, and its members stand by each other in times of trouble. In the course of the plot he finds himself in a "jungle": surrounded by power-hungry people who will not stop in their quest to gain even more power, with little concern for other people. *Castle in the Sky*, however, made the character of the civilized boy far more realistic and complex: Pazu is not a perfect person; he has his doubts, and at one point even seems on the verge of giving up on his quest and leaving Sheeta behind. *Castle in the Sky* also gives a far more pessimistic view toward the ability of the civilized boy to educate the other characters in the social "jungle" that he finds himself in; though he succeeds in preventing Muska and his gang from using Laputa for their ends, they are merely defeated and none of them sees anything wrong with what he does all the way to the film's end.

Sheeta also carries on the tradition of female characters from Miyazaki's previous works, going all the way back to *Gulliver's Travels Beyond the Moon*. Like the princess of the robots' planet in the early Tōei feature, who shed her robotic shell to reveal the human inside, Sheeta leaves behind her high-class status of noble and even royal ancestry, finding life among the common folk—especially the miners' community from which Pazu came—a far more ideal form of living. Unlike

Nausicaa—a friend to the common folk who nonetheless retains her status as their birthright leader—Sheeta goes all the way in her wish to live life as an equal among others.

Another element related to female characters from Miyazaki's previous works that found its way to Sheeta is the family secret that these characters hold. Kathy of *Animal Treasure Island* and Clarice of *The Castle of Cagliostro* had the knowledge of an ancient treasure buried by their ancestors, Lana of *Future Boy Conan* could lead the way to a distant legendary region from which she came, and Princess Rastel (a minor character from *Nausicaa of the Valley of the Wind*) held a family heirloom that can bring doom upon mankind. Like all these characters, Sheeta's royal heritage brings her to the possession of a potentially deadly secret, related to the flying island and its powers. The social consciousness that Sheeta develops during the film's plot, her realization that she wants nothing to do with the life of nobility or royalty, also makes her understand how important the secret she guards is, and how dangerous it can be if it falls into the wrong hands.

Finally, Sheeta is also reminiscent of the heroines of the *Calpis/World Masterpiece Theatre* productions, Heidi in particular, in the sense that she grows and develops over the course of the film. At the beginning, she is a scared girl, trapped in the high-society circle that surrounds her (evident in the film's opening scene, showing her being delivered by government agents aboard a luxury airship). As the plot progresses, she gains confidence from the time she spends with the rural community, fueling her rebelliousness against the same high-society circle—not unlike Heidi's ideal time in the Alps' village among the common peasants, contrasted with her miserable life in the city among the high-class urban society.

Minor characters also echo elements from Miyazaki's earlier works, and works that inspired Miyazaki. Especially notable is Dolla, the leader of the air-pirates' gang, who combines elements from both the wise old woman archetype—which originated in Atamanov's *The Snow Queen* and found its way to Miyazaki's work on *Heidi of the Alps* and *Nausicaa of the Valley of the Wind*—and the leader of the bandits' gang, also from Atamanov's film. While in *The Snow Queen* the leader of the bandits' gang was an antagonist, Miyazaki has made Dolla a hero who helps the protagonists in *Castle in the Sky*. Set against the social backdrop that inspired the film, Dolla and her gang are not only a group of greedy thieves but also heroic anarchists who oppose those in power. Combined with the wisdom of the wise old woman, Miyazaki has made Dolla a new kind of female role-model for his audience, one who shows that rebelliousness against oppression can very much be a part of life in old-age too.

Muska, the villain of *Castle in the Sky*, is also cast from the same mold of characters from Miyazaki's previous works, and the inspiration for his character can in fact be traced to that of the evil king from Grimault's *The Shepherdess and the Chimney Sweep*—a power-hungry monarch who seeks not just further means of oppression but also a spouse who can provide him with heirs to carry on his lineage. In Grimault's film, the evil king set his sights on the working-class Shepherdess, not understanding why she resists his offer to rise up to a higher social status. This inspired both the kidnapping of Princess Rosa by the Lucifer of Tōei's *Puss 'n Boots* and the marriage that Count Cagliostro attempted to force Clarice into in *Castle of Cagliostro*. The difference is that, in both cases, the antagonists saw marriage to the princess as a way to upgrade their own social status (ensuring their reign of the kingdom) while in Grimault's film the evil king stands to gain no such upgrade—he sees the low-class Shepherdess as merely another object that can be added to his treasure. The relationship between Muska and Sheeta is closer, in this respect, to those seen in *The Shepherdess and the Chimney Sweep*: like the Shepherdess, Sheeta rejects Muska's offer to be uplifted to a higher social status and rule beside him, not only because (as noted above) she finds life among the common folk ideal, but also because she knows that his reign will be a reign of terror.

Muska's character also strongly resembles (in both design and behavior) the character of Lepka, the ruthless commander of Industria's army in *Future Boy Conan*. Much like Lepka—or, for that matter, Lucifer and Count Cagliostro—Muska is eventually a rather one-dimensional villain character, of the kind that indeed typified Miyazaki's earlier works, but was not seen in the films that followed *Castle in the Sky*.

Locations in the film also combine elements from Miyazaki's past works and works that inspired him. The town of the hard-working miners, as noted above, was inspired by Miyazaki's trip to Wales but it also echoes the agricultural communities seen in *Heidi of the Alps*, *Anne of Green Gables*, and Back's *Crac!*. An even more direct influence appears to have come from the "Where Did the Sovereigns Go?" episode of *Sherlock Hound*. As noted in Chapter 3, the episode also presented a town whose people live in poverty (and also featured pseudo-British backgrounds), and the geographical layout is also very similar—just like the people of the town in the *Sherlock Hound* episode were living in the shadow of the industrialist's luxurious castle, the people of the miners' town in *Castle in the Sky* live in the shadow of an intimidating army-fortress operated by the government. The geographical relationship in *Castle in the Sky* reflects more of an anti-fascist sentiment rather than the anti-capitalist sentiment of "Where Did the Sovereigns Go?" and this sentiment is actually closer to Grimault's film, which (as noted in Chapter 3) inspired the episode.

Grimault's film also strongly inspired the fantasy setting of the flying island and its many wonders, a setting that also combines elements from Miyazaki's past works and other works that influenced him into a wonderfully solid vision. Laputa, as seen in the film, is very much a multi-layered location with a surface of beautiful ever-green gardens but also many dark tunnels and secret passages hidden underneath, not unlike the evil king's castle in *The Shepherdess and the Chimney Sweep*. But it is also an eerily silent place, abandoned, much like the evil king's entire kingdom in Grimault's film, and the abandoned mines that Miyazaki saw on his trip to Wales (a sight that, like the kingdom in Grimault's film, represents the cruelty of the regime toward the people). It also brings to mind the forbidden paradise motif from the *Star Blazers* franchise that Miyazaki has already referred to in *Nausicaa of the Valley of the Wind*—in *Castle in the Sky* this paradise also awaits its female resident to come to it and stay, possibly even rule it, yet this female resident (Sheeta, much like Nausicaa) rejects this fate.

The sense of Laputa being a forbidden paradise is emphasized in the film through its residents—a group of giant robots that tend its gardens. Here Miyazaki makes another reference to the soulless robots from *Gulliver's Travels Beyond the Moon* (and in another reference, the robots of Laputa also treat a female character as their master), and also to the giant robots from Grimault's film and those from the Fleischers' *Mechanical Monsters* (and the references he made to these robots in previous works such as *The Flying Ghost Ship* and "Farewell, Beloved Lupin")—again, tools of terror and destruction in the hand of a greedy and power-hungry individual. At the same time, these robots show another side—they are also the guardians of the flying island, who tend its gardens and can be used for peaceful and positive ends. Here, Miyazaki appears to have drawn further inspiration from *Silent Running* (discussed in the previous chapter as an influence on *Nausicaa of the Valley of the Wind*)—Trumbull's film also featured robots that tend gardens on flying platforms. The shot of the heroes leaving Laputa, shortly before the end of *Castle in the Sky*, is a direct homage to the final shot of *Silent Running*,

The design of the giant robots in *Castle in the Sky* showcase the influence of many productions that Miyazaki has worked on over the years, such as *Gulliver's Space Travels* and *The Flying Ghost Ship*, alongside the inspiration he drew from foreign productions, such as the Fleischer brothers' *Mechanical Monsters* and Paul Grimault's *The Adventures of Mr. Wonderbird*.

showing a garden floating in space, tended by a robot. While works by Grimault and the Fleischer brothers inspired the portrayal of the darker sides of the flying island, Douglas Trumbull's film inspired the positive representations of potential technological developments in *Castle in the Sky*, showing how technology can exist harmoniously with nature and the environment.[5]

Castle in the Sky also shows several new sources of influence, literary and cinematic, some contemporary to the time of the film's debut and some of more classic status. The flying island's name, Laputa, is the name of the flying island in Jonathan Swift's 1726 satirical literary masterpiece *Gulliver's Travels*, which of course had already inspired *Gulliver's Travels Beyond the Moon*. Unlike the Tōei production, *Castle in the Sky* makes no reference to either the characters or the plot of Swift's novel, and in fact explains (in a dialogue between Pazu and Sheeta), that the island described by Swift is "fictional" as opposed to the "real" flying island in the film's world. But while he makes no references to the novel other than the island's name (which caused something of a problem upon the film's North American release, as the phrase "la puta" means "whore" in Spanish[6]) and its nature, there is a strong thematic link between the two works: the people of Swift's novel's Laputa are intellectuals detached from the everyday lives of the people below, and sometimes terrorize these people with the great power their island possesses, bombarding them with rocks. The people of Laputa in Miyazaki's film chose to leave the island and come down to Earth in order to avoid such a fate (as explained by Sheeta in the film); to become a part of the human race, not superior to it. Muska's attempt to restore what he believes to be the former glory of the flying island is—beyond an evil plan—also a laughable attempt at placing oneself above all other people, the very kind of attempt mocked by Swift himself. Artistic representations of Swift's Laputa, and their influence on later fantasy and science fiction art echo in Miyazaki's film, especially the classic nineteenth-century illustrations of the novel by French artist Jean Ignace Isidore Gérard that portrayed Swift's flying island as a fortress on a round flying platform.[7]

Another work that strongly influenced *Castle in the Sky* is *Journey to the Center of the Earth*, Henry Levin's 1959 Hollywood adaptation of the classic adventure novel by Jules Verne, following a group of explorers who go on a quest to discover the secrets hidden deep underneath Earth's surface. At least two scenes from Levin's film are given a direct reference in *Castle in the Sky*: one features a dark cave that is suddenly lit due to the presence of mysterious crystals, and the other shows a passage through an electric storm eventually leading the protagonists to an ancient hidden kingdom. The hidden kingdom, which in Levin's film turns out to be the lost continent Atlantis, is an abandoned place, the remains of a once-great culture whose time has passed, not unlike Miyazaki's Laputa. *Journey to the Center of the Earth* also provided strong inspiration for both George Lucas and Steven Spielberg[8] as they were re-inventing the adventure film genre for Hollywood at the time *Castle in the Sky* came out, and the work of both filmmakers left its mark on Miyazaki as well: the plot of his film, following heroes on a race to prevent an ancient and potentially dangerous treasure from falling into evil hands, will feel familiar to anyone who saw Spielberg's *Raiders of the Lost Ark*, while Lucas' *Star Wars* gets direct visual references in Laputa's Death Star-like inner structure and deadly powers (including a completely similar firing pattern).

Many years after its release, *Castle in the Sky* was widely recognized as a seminal work in the genre that came to be known as Steampunk—a wide term bringing together works of literature, film, art, music, and fashion that feature a retro-futuristic style reminiscent of nineteenth-century science fiction.[9] Other than its retro aesthetic, Miyazaki's film also celebrates an important deeper theme common in the genre—the emphasis on home-made technology, the wondrous vehicles and gadgets built by the aspiring inventors in their own home with their own tools. Pazu and Dolla's gang use this kind of technology, with the loving touch of gifted people's creativity, which is so different from the big, ugly machines used by Muska and his men. Miyazaki, in his proposal for the film, made a special note of his wish to focus on home-made technology, obviously seen by him as another expression of individual freedom.[10]

For all the inspiration it drew from Miyazaki's past two decades in the animation industry and its deeper themes of the fight against oppression, the greatest achievement of *Castle in the Sky* is perhaps the fact that it can be considered one of the greatest adventure films ever made. Miyazaki's following feature films, while also drawing inspiration from his past works, went in decidedly different directions.

Growing up in a Happy Past

As discussed earlier in this chapter, *Castle in the Sky* was heavily inspired by action-oriented productions involving Miyazaki during his early career, while also drawing some inspiration for its pseudo-European scenery from the *Calpis/World Masterpiece Theatre* productions. In the following two films directed by Miyazaki at Studio Ghibli, *My Neighbor Totoro* (*Tonari no Totoro*, 1988) and *Kiki's Delivery Service* (*Majo no Takkyūbin*, 1989), the *Calpis/World Masterpiece Theatre* productions became the main source of influence, and this influence went deeper beyond superficial visual similarities. Both films celebrate the joy of everyday life, with no violence and very little conflict, and focus on the passage from childhood to adulthood in an ideal manner. Both films are also far more personal works than the three features directed by Miyazaki before them; they reflect both his childhood experiences and the long way he has come since the beginning of his career as an animator.

My Neighbor Totoro is set in rural Japan of the 1950s, following nine-year-old Satsuki and her four-year-old sister Mei as they move with their father to a small rural village, close to the hospital where their mother is being treated for an illness. Though the move to the new house and new surroundings brings many exciting discoveries for both protagonists, their mother's deteriorating health always casts a shadow on their happiness. They overcome their fears through their friendship with Totoro—a strange creature who lives in the wild forest near their house.

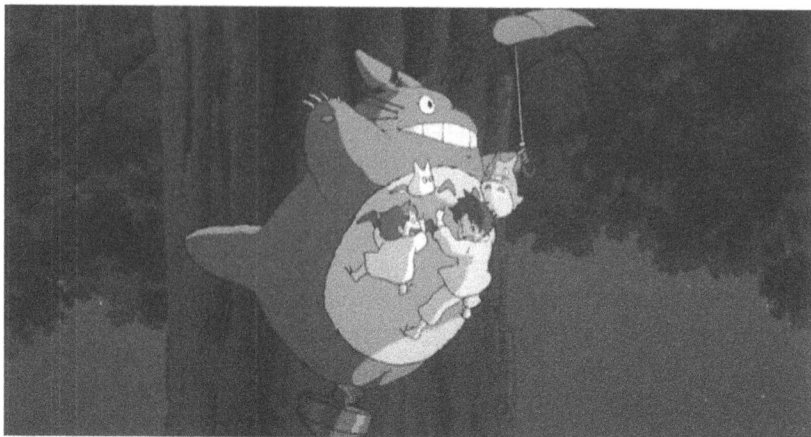

In directing *My Neighbor Totoro*, Miyazaki drew on his experience from working on two realistic productions that emphasize the day-to-day lives of young girls, *Heidi, Girl of the Alps* and *Anne of the Green Gables*, and from his work on productions that linked childhood and fantasy, such as *Moomins* and *Panda! Go Panda!*

Based on a children's book by Japanese author Eiko Kadono, *Kiki's Delivery Service* also takes place in the 1950s, though not in historical Japan but rather in an idealized version of Europe in the same era. In an unnamed European country where World War II never occurred and magic is real, young witch Kiki must leave her home in the village upon turning thirteen and spend a year away from her family. She arrives at the big city of Koriko, attempting to find her place in it, and goes through many adventures while attempting to open a flying delivery-service.

My Neighbor Totoro is a film that celebrates the joys of childhood in a manner deeply inspired by the *Calpis/World Masterpiece Theatre* productions and their predecessors. *Heidi*, in particular, echoes in the film's opening scenes that link joyous childhood and wild nature: like Heidi, upon arriving at their new house in a rural environment, both Satsuki and Mei run around in the front yard, which is very much a geographical reflection of young age; like the natural landscapes that surround the village in the Alps, it is a place where grass and flowers grow with no sign of the tending hand of a gardener, leading to a forest of wild-growing ancient trees—a place that represents the freedom to grow and express one's emotions without disturbance. It is in these forests that Mei happily gets lost, free from the rules of time and space of the adult world.

The world of happy childhood, unbound by such rules, allows the film's protagonists to step completely outside the boundaries of reality into the realm of fantasy, meeting Totoro and his family of smaller similar creatures who, like Totoro himself, are designed in a manner that combines the look of a cat, tanuki (Japanese raccoon), and an owl. Unsurprisingly, Totoro's home is in the same wild, untamed forest that Mei adores[11]; its design recalls the size of the great Panda bear from *Panda! Go Panda!* and also the roundness of the trolls from *Moomins*— in fact, considering Miyazaki's rather brief involvement with the production of the *Moomins*, the inspiration he drew from it while working on *My Neighbor Totoro* is considerable, from the very name Mei gives Totoro (mispronouncing the word "Troll" from a book her mother read her) to the casting of Hitoshi Takagi—who voiced Moominpapa, the head of the Moomin family, in the animated adaptation. Miyazaki's brief involvement with *Little Nemo: Adventures in Slumberland* also inspired one of the most breathtaking fantasy sequences in *My Neighbor Totoro*, in which Totoro takes both Mei and Satsuki on an epic flight during the night, recalling the flight of the protagonist from Yoshifumi Kondō's pilot film, leaving the protagonists to debate the following morning whether this flight really happened, or if they just had a dream. This sequence also shows the influence of contemporary Hollywood cinema on Miyazaki: much like *Castle in the Sky*, *My Neighbor Totoro* also makes references to director Steven Spielberg, especially to *E.T. the Extra-Terrestrial* (1982) in the moonlight flight, the initial discovery of Totoro by Mei, and the general plot of children befriending a strange creature in the wake of a family crisis.

But childhood is not just joy; it also has its shares of fears and doubts. As noted above, the excitement and happiness in the discovery of the film's protagonists' new surroundings is marred by their fear for their mother's health. As noted in the first chapter, there is a strong autobiographical element in the protagonists' fear of orphanhood, as Miyazaki saw his own mother struggle with a disease that threatened her life during his own childhood. This experience has already been channeled into Miyazaki's earlier work on *3,000 Leagues in Search of Mother* and, as in the show, the threat of orphanhood confronts the protagonists of *My Neighbor Totoro* with the adult world. Satsuki, in particular, is something of a tragic figure in the film, old enough to realize the possible implications of her mother's illness and forced to grow up too fast due to this realization. In the course of the film, Satsuki takes upon herself her absent mother's responsibilities of housework and cooking, and also the more metaphysical adult responsibilities of space and time; unlike her little sister, who easily and happily gets lost and has little sense of time (Mei's most distant idea of future time is "tomorrow"), Satsuki has an excellent sense of direction and quickly finds her way. She is also very aware (and makes the audience aware) of the time that passes through letters written by her to her mother in the hospital—and these letters emphasize the changing of seasons and the passing of days, weeks, and months. Such control over time was also featured in the *Panda! Go Panda!* films, where the audience was also made aware of the passing time through letters written by Mimiko to her grandmother.[12]

Over the course of the film, as Satsuki is drawn deeper into the adult world, she starts growing apart from her sister. The divide between the two characters is made explicit through their design: Satsuki's design is realistic and basically presents her as a younger version of the film's adult characters, while Mei's design is far more cartoon-like, as is evident in her big head (slightly disproportional to the rest of her body) and her exaggerated gestures, recalling both Mimiko from the *Panda! Go Panda!* films (especially the pigtails hairstyle) and the little girl who approached Holmes for help in "A Small Client."[13] This design makes Mei stand out in the society that surrounds her: in a sense, Mei is the only real child in the entire film, as no other characters of the same age are seen, and the slightly older characters (like Satsuki) are basically young adults. Satsuki, on the other hand, is surrounded by other children her age and is somewhat embarrassed by Mei's behavior in their presence (echoing the relationship between two other sisters from an earlier work that involved Miyazaki—Diana and Minnie-Mei from *Anne of Green Gables*). Not unlike Heidi or Anne, who compensated the lack of parents with integration into the society that surrounds them, Satsuki also integrates quickly into society and moves away from her family.

But, unlike Heidi or Anne, Satsuki is not an orphan, but rather a child who lives under the threat of orphanhood. Like Marco of *3,000 Leagues in Search of Mother*, Satsuki attempts to put on a brave face in reaction to this threat, but the quick growing-up process that she experiences is a painful one. While Mei, in the absence of her mother, relies on her sister to guide her through the adult world that she does not understand, Satsuki turns to Mei's childhood fantasy of Totoro to gain mental strength, to forget about the troubles of the adult world. In the film's climax, when Satsuki and Mei are told that their mother's condition has worsened, Satsuki finally breaks down in tears, confessing to the elderly woman who lives nearby her house (a wise old woman, of the kind already seen in both *Nausicaa of the Valley of the Wind* and *Castle in the Sky*) about her fears. Mei, who witnesses her sister's condition, realizes that Satsuki can no longer provide her with the support and confidence she needs, and decides to go to the hospital and make sure her mother is well. After Mei gets lost, Satsuki discovers that she cannot find Mei with the help of representatives from the adult society that she sunk into; only by asking Totoro, the embodiment of Mei's childhood fantasy, for help does Satsuki manage to find Mei and arrive at the hospital where both sisters discover their mother is fine.

Childhood cannot last forever, and even though the film's closing credits show the protagonists' mother's happy return, they also show Satsuki continuing her passage from the childhood world of family to the adult world of society, and Mei beginning her own similar passage as she is shown playing with other children. What are not seen in the closing titles are scenes featuring either Satsuki or Mei with Totoro—both characters slowly move away from their childhood fantasy, now that they have relied on it to overcome the emotional crisis they went through. There is a sense of sadness in this farewell to the world of childhood, but the world of adults and the passage to it is not portrayed in a negative manner in *My Neighbor Totoro*; the film hints that this world offers its own ideal living. Alongside the wild forests that represent childhood's lack of time and space, *My Neighbor Totoro* also shows man-made gardens and large agricultural fields, an ideal living by people who co-exist with nature much like the people seen in *Castle in the Sky* and in Back's *Crac!*.

Kiki's Delivery Service picked up where *My Neighbor Totoro* left off, focusing on the magic of growing up. If the protagonists of *My Neighbor Totoro* faced the threat of orphanhood, it can be said that the protagonist of *Kiki's Delivery Service* chooses orphanhood. The film opens with her decision to leave behind her family and all the people of her village (who serve as an extended family for her—the film emphasizes how everyone in the village knows Kiki and all come to bid her farewell) and make the passage into society. This passage from childhood to adulthood uses the same metaphor from *Heidi, Girl of the Alps* as it is presented as a passage from the village to the city. But while the city of Frankfurt in *Heidi, Girl of the Alps* was presented as a cold, dark, and serious place devoid of any joy, the fictional city of Koriko in *Kiki's Delivery Service* is nothing short of an urban paradise. The main influence on the city's design was the Swedish city of Visby, which Miyazaki had visited almost two decades earlier when he was sent for the failed negotiations over the rights to

Kiki's Delivery Service celebrates Miyazaki's love for European landscapes that he absorbed during his work on productions such as *Heidi, Girl of the Alps*, *3,000 Leagues in Search of Mother*, and the unproduced adaptation of *Pippi Longstocking*.

Pippi Longstocking, and where he took the production staff of *Kiki's Delivery Service* for a research trip.[14] It is presented as a place where middle- and upper-class citizens lead happy and productive lives, contributing to greater society by both working and raising their families. At the beginning of the film, Kiki is excited about integrating into this utopian society, but shortly afterwards she discovers that it will not be as easy as she initially thought.

    Kiki's Delivery Service corresponds with the popular "Magical Girl" genre of Japanese comics and animation, a genre that Miyazaki had worked on in one of its pioneering productions *Sally the Witch* (discussed in Chapter 1). While typical works of the genre emphasize individuality and uniqueness of their protagonists who stand above the non-magical population and whose integration into this population is merely a façade for their true identity, *Kiki's Delivery Service* is all about a true integration into society—the hard process of making society accept newcomers, and the equally hard process of going through the necessary personal changes to fit within society. In this sense, Kiki has more in common with Anne of *Anne of Green Gables* than with Sally or the protagonist of any subsequent magical girl production: like the red-haired girl from the *World Masterpiece Theatre* show, Kiki is also very enthusiastic about coming to a new place, but initially expects that this place will accept her and her strong individual personality as they are; the growing-up process that she goes through teaches her that she, too, has to adjust in order to fit into society.

Nowhere is this more evident than in one of the film's most delightful scenes in which Kiki, shortly after her arrival at the city, flies on her broom in an extravagant manner to show off her skill and almost causes a traffic accident. The scared people in the street run away and an angry cop quickly shows up to shout at her. This scene demonstrates the influence of Yoshifumi Kondō—who returned to work with Miyazaki and joined Studio Ghibli when *Kiki's Delivery Service* went into production—and there is more than a passing resemblance between the exciting but highly dangerous flight sequence from the pilot film that Kondō directed for *Little Nemo: Adventures in Slumberland* and the almost-disaster that Kiki causes in her flight. The first impression Kiki makes on her new surroundings is not as positive as she hoped—yet she fails to realize at this point that she is responsible for this impression, and that she needs to fit in rather than thinking that she is above everyone else.

This process of fitting into society involves another aspect of growing up, the discovery of the opposite sex. Shortly after being scolded by the policeman, Kiki is approached by Tombo, a boy her age with a passion for flying, who falls utterly in love with her upon seeing her flying on her broom. Tombo's initial attempts at winning Kiki's friendship are met with stubborn rejections—as much as Kiki is fascinated by the world of adults, one side of it, the realization that one day she will find a man and start her own family (giving up something of her individual existence) scares her. This aspect of Kiki's personality is reminiscent of Anne's relationship with Gilbert Blythe and also of a minor plot in *My Neighbor Totoro* in which Satsuki draws the attention of a local boy named Kanta (who is also a fan of airplanes) and, while the two are initially hostile to one another, they grow closer as the plot progresses. Of course, since the characters of *My Neighbor Totoro* are much younger, Satsuki and Kanta's relationship is far less significant than that of Kiki and Tombo.

Fortunately for Kiki, she soon finds herself surrounded by other characters that both guide her on her way to successful integration into adult society and provide positive role models to follow. First among them is Ursula, an artist who is only a few years older than Kiki herself, who serves as a big sister of sorts (recalling the relationship between Satsuki and Mei), and teaches Kiki about finding what makes her unique. Then comes Osono, a young married woman expecting her first child and the owner of a bakery who provides Kiki with a place to live. In

Osono, Kiki sees a person who shaped her unique talents into something that serves as part of a large, functioning society. Finally, there is the wise old woman, familiar from Miyazaki's previous works, now in the form of an elderly lady for whom Kiki performs deliveries, who can look back satisfied at a lifetime of successful integration into society. This ideal introduction of an individual into an ideal society in many ways reflects Miyazaki's own experiences in the animation industry, from the beginning of his career as a junior animator to his peak as a prominent director.

But in *Kiki's Delivery Service*, this introduction is performed exclusively by female characters. The film is, above all, a grand celebration of femininity, not unlike *Nausicaa of the Valley of the Wind*. While Miyazaki's manga and its animated adaptation presented female leadership as an alternative to wars and destruction, *Kiki's Delivery Service* presents women as those who keep society functioning in an ideal manner. By the time he worked on the film, Miyazaki had over two decades' worth of strong female characters to inspire him—both in the works of others that influenced him and in the works he was involved with.

Notes

1 Ōtsuka, *Sakuga Asemamire*, 205–209.
2 Kanō, *Nippon no Animation o Kizuita Hitobito*, 32–33.
3 This assumption is based on Miyazaki's review of Back's *The Man Who Planted Trees*, originally published in 1988, in which he mentions seeing *Crac!* For the first time during a visit to the United States "for work, four or five years ago"—roughly the same period in which he worked on *Little Nemo: Adventures in Slumberland*. See Miyazaki, *Starting Point*, 143–146.
4 McCarthy, *Hayao Miyazaki, Master of Japanese Animation*, 95–96.
5 For a discussion of the themes in Trumbull's film, see Mark Kermode, *Silent Running* (London: BFI, 2014).
6 McCarthy, *Hayao Miyazaki, Master of Japanese Animation*, 96.
7 Interestingly, Gerard's illustration, which became the popular visualization of Swift's Laputa, also had a longstanding influence on modern fantasy illustrations, from American science fiction author Frank R. Paul in a classic cover for *Air Wonder Stories Magazine* (November 1929) to the designers of the alien ship in the second *Space Battleship Yamato* film, *Farewell to Battleship Yamato* (1978)—which might have provided Miyazaki with an even more direct visual influence. Another famous visual interpretation of Swift's novel—the Fleischer brothers' feature-length film, which also inspired *Gullivers' Travels Beyond the Moon*—is not directly referenced in *Castle in the Sky*, but the film's extremely negative portrayal

of war and warmongers definitely shows influence on the characters of
Muska and the army men that surround him in Miyazaki's film.

8   Kristen Brennan, "Other Science Fiction," *Star Wars Origins* (2006).
    Available online: http://moongadget.com/origins/general.html

9   Jeff Vandermeer and S.J. Chambers, *The Steampunk Bible* (New York:
    Abrams Image, 2012), 186–187.

10 Miyazaki, *Starting Point*, 252–254. Interestingly, *Sherlock Hound*, which
    took place in a pseudo-Victorian setting, also featured many innovative
    machines that were products of either private entrepreneurship or
    home-modifications. Such technologies, however, were not necessarily
    used in the show for positive purposes (often being tools in the hand of
    the protagonist's nemesis Moriarty).

11 The scenery of both the *Panda! Go Panda!* films and *My Neighbor Totoro*
    was partially inspired by the area that surrounds the city of Tokorozawa,
    where Miyazaki lives (Clements and McCarthy, *The Anime Encyclopedia*,
    1908–1909).

12 The analysis presented here on *My Neighbor Totoro* is based and expands
    on an article by me published in the *Literature Film Quarterly* journal. See
    Greenberg, "Giri and Ninjo," 96–108.

13 Interestingly, *My Neighbor Totoro* was originally meant to feature only a
    single protagonist, and early promotional posters for the film still feature
    this single character—which looks like a mixture of the design of both
    Satsuki and Mei. See Hayao Miyazaki, *The Art of My Neighbor Totoro* (San
    Francisco: Viz Media, 2005), 7–11.

14 In another connection to Lindgren's novel, initial designs sketched for
    Kiki's character presented her as a red-haired girl with pigtails, much like
    Pippi. See Hayao Miyazaki, *The Art of Kiki's Delivery Service* (San
    Francisco: Viz Media, 2006), 11, 67. Additional inspiration may have come
    from an experience described by Miyazaki of his first visit to Stockholm,
    seeing a "witch-like woman dragging a bag," in one of the city's streets early
    in the morning, who upon closer inspection turned out to be "an old
    woman delivering papers" (Takahata, Miyazaki, and Kotabe, *Maboroshi no
    Nagagutsu no Pippi*, 66–67).

Chapter 6

GROWING OLD IN AN UNCERTAIN PRESENT

Kiki's Delivery Service became Studio Ghibli's first true commercial hit, becoming the most successful domestic film at Japan's box-office in 1989,[1] an achievement that each of Miyazaki's subsequent films would repeat. Miyazaki was not the only person to direct films at Studio Ghibli; Takahata helmed both *Grave of the Fireflies* (*Hotaru no haka*, 1988), which follows the struggle for survival of two children during the bombings of Japan in World War II and *Only Yesterday* (*Omoide Poro Poro*, 1991), a contemporary drama about a Tokyo career woman who goes on vacation and through the memories of her past tries to understand where her life is heading. Like Miyazaki, Takahata drew on his experience from working on the different *Calpis/World Masterpiece Theatre* shows, but while Miyazaki borrowed different elements from these shows for films that were framed with a strong fantasy setting, Takahata was mostly inspired by these shows' realistic nature, commenting about the world in a more direct and less metaphorical manner than Miyazaki did in his films. However, Takahata's later films at Studio Ghibli, *Pom Poko* (*Heisei Tanuki Gassen Ponpoko*, 1994), *My Neighbors the Yamadas* (*Tonari no Yamada-kun*, 1999), and *The Tale of Princess Kaguya* (*Kaguya-hime no Monogtari*, 2013) were more fantastic in nature—and though each of his Studio Ghibli films was interesting in its own right, it is hard to discuss his entire body of work as one of consistent, personal style, like Miyazaki's.

Another noteworthy non-Miyazaki film directed at Studio Ghibli is *Whisper of the Heart* (*Mimi wo Sumaseba*, 1995). Adapted from a manga by artist Aoi Hiragi, the film follows Shizuku, a young girl who dreams of becoming a writer while trying to figure out her relationship with Seiji, a boy from her school. Directed by Yoshifumi Kondō and based on a script by Miyazaki, the film is notable for its colorful dream sequence—again, very reminiscent of Kondō's work on the pilot for

Little Nemo: Adventures in Slumberland—but, although providing a pleasant viewing experience, *Whisper of the Heart* feels more like a recycling of themes from Miyazaki's optimistic films throughout the 1980s. By the time the film came out, Miyazaki's own directorial work took a decidedly more somber tone.

This tone reflects the uncertainty that Miyazaki must have felt as the 1980s came to a close, with the new decade marked by the collapse of Japan's bubble-economy and the prosperity that influenced the happy mood of his previous films (though, ironically, also marked by the great financial success that Miyazaki's films found in the Japanese box-office), alongside the collapse of the Soviet Union, which made Miyazaki reconsider his core beliefs as a radical leftist. Such uncertainty marks Miyazaki's first feature in the 1990s, *Porco Rosso* (*Kurenai no Buta*, 1992). The film's protagonist, Marco Pagot, is a former World War I fighter pilot who is deeply bitter about his homeland turning fascist, becoming a humanoid pig. Even in this state, Marco remains a top-flying ace, working as a bounty hunter against a gang of air-pirates that terrorize the skies of the Adriatic Sea in the late 1920s. Though Marco easily has the upper hand in his struggle against the gang, things change when cocky American pilot Donald Curtis enters the picture, and when both Marco's young mechanic Fio and his old flame Gina attempt to persuade him that there is still hope for both him and humanity.

Porco Rosso is a film of contrasts, marking a transitional period in both Miyazaki's career and the state of world affairs. The film contains some of the funniest scenes ever directed by Miyazaki, but they are often followed by serious, downbeat moments that remind viewers of the dark period during which the film takes place, and the even darker times that will follow. Nowhere in the film is this contrast more obvious than in a charming scene taking place in an Italian movie theatre, where Marco watches a film with an old comrade named Ferrarin. The film they watch is a black and white cartoon in the style of early American animation. It begins as a homage to Walt Disney's 1928 film *Plane Crazy*, the first film produced starring the character of Mickey Mouse (although released after the subsequently produced *Steamboat Willie* of the same year). Much like *Porco Rosso*, *Plane Crazy* also deals with the construction of an airplane, and makes fun of the well-oiled machine ideal they represent (both films end with the complete destruction of the airplanes constructed in them, albeit under different circumstances). Another famous cartoon character from the era, Max Fleischer's Betty Boop, soon joins the Mickey Mouse-like protagonist on the screen, and later a

Winsor McCay-style dinosaur character (a reference to McCay's famous *Gertie the Dinosaur* performances) and a pig character reminiscent of Disney's 1933 film *Three Little Pigs* (another poke at the plot of *Porco Rosso*) are also seen. While Marco and his old comrade Ferrarin enjoy the show, their conversation soon turns grim as they discuss the fascist regime, and as Marco leaves the theatre, catching a ride with Fio, he is followed by the secret police.

The film's conflicting elements can be traced to its origins—first as a manga titled *Hikaōtei Jidai* (*Crimson Pig: The Age of Flying Boat*) drawn by Miyazaki in 1990 and published in 1992. A short affair compared with Miyazaki's previous epic-proportions of *Nausicaa of the Valley of the Wind* manga, *Crimson Pig: The Age of Flying Boat* consists of three five-page chapters that, much like the later anime film, follow the adventures of a humanoid-pig named Marco and his struggle against air pirates in the Adriatic skies of the late 1920s.[2] In fact, much of the narrative frame from the manga found its way to the film: the initial fight between Marco and the pirates' gang, which involves a heroic rescue of a young girl, the dogfight between Marco and the gang's new champion who is a cocky American pilot (named "Donald Chuck" in the manga) ending with Marco being shot down, the repairs of Marco's plane in a small workshop operated by a large Italian family, and the friendship that develops between Marco and the youngest member of the family—a young mechanic named Fio, all leading to the final showdown between Marco and Donald, starting as an aerial battle and ending in a fistfight from which Marco emerges victorious.

At the same time, the tone and focus of the manga are very different from those of the film. While *Porco Rosso*, as noted above, balances its comedic scenes with serious drama, *Crimson Pig: The Age of Flying Boat* is played almost strictly for laughs: not only does it feature the physical and verbal gags that the film retained, but it also breaks the fourth wall on an almost regular basis, often referring to the fact that the manga is too short for a complete showcase of the aerial fights so readers will have to guess what happened between the beginning of a battle and its resolution. Politics of the 1920s are referred to in the manga, but they do not play any significant role. Initially, the film version of the story was meant to be much closer to the manga. Miyazaki's original plans were for a short animated comedy, played during airline flights. But as work progressed and different political changes shook the world and Japan, Miyazaki realized that through an expansion of original manga's vision, he could make a serious commentary.[3]

This commentary is very evident in the manner in which *Porco Rosso* refers to Miyazaki's earlier filmography. The very idea of an anthropomorphic pig character dates back to Miyazaki's own work on *Animal Treasure Island*, where such a character led the pirates' gang. In *Porco Rosso*, Marco is of course the film's protagonist rather than antagonist, and is in conflict with a pirates' gang, but he does share a few things with the character from the earlier film other than design, especially the (sometimes misguided) confidence in his ability to win any confrontation he gets involved with. The pirates' gang in *Animal Treasure Island* also strongly influenced the gang from *Porco Rosso*—while not consisting of anthropomorphic characters as in the earlier film, it is a group of none-too-clever misfits who are eventually portrayed as more funny than dangerous. But while the struggle against the pirates in *Animal Treasure Island* was portrayed as something significant, standing at the heart of the film's plot, *Porco Rosso* clarifies that Marco's struggle against the pirates' gang is an event of minor significance compared with the quickly-deteriorating state of affairs that surrounds the characters, and even the sheer anarchy it creates can do nothing against the rise of fascism. The characters of *Porco Rosso* fight in the air and with their fists over money, honor, and love, while being helpless against the greater evil that slowly grows around them.

Marco also shares his name with another protagonist of an earlier work that involved Miyazaki—*3,000 Leagues in Search of Mother*. Like the show's protagonist, Marco of *Porco Rosso* is also from Genoa, and also befriends a young girl named Fio (Fiorina in *3,000 Leagues in Search of Mother* is the youngest daughter of the puppet-theatre manager). Again, the influence of Miyazaki's earlier work on the show gets a bitter twist in *Porco Rosso*: De Amicis' story, which provided the inspiration for the show, dealt with the hopes and dreams of the citizens of Italy when it was a young modern state, and how these hopes and dreams helped them cope with economic hardships; the series, in its opening chapters, demonstrated these hopes and dreams as well. In *Porco Rosso*, viewers are reminded of how these hopes and dreams turned into nightmares as Italian nationalism turned into militant dictatorship. Marco, the brave and kind-hearted boy who never lost faith in people from *3,000 Leagues in Search of Mother*, became Marco—the aging pilot from *Porco Rosso* who is also brave and kind-hearted, but also deeply cynical, having lost his faith in people.

"The White Cliffs of Dover" episode from *Sherlock Hound* was another early work by Miyazaki that served as an important source of inspiration for *Porco Rosso*. The portrayal of Mrs. Hudson's character in this episode—a pilot's widow who comes to the aid of her late husband's colleagues in the face of danger, and who remains a strong and optimistic person despite her loss—is a clear influence on the portrayal of the character of Gina in *Porco Rosso*. Again, the influence of the earlier work is framed by a more complex and realistic political background; while Mrs. Hudson manages to save the entire Royal Air Mail service, Gina cannot and does not aspire to save her entire country from fascism. She does succeed, though, in restoring Marco's faith in humanity and love— like the younger character of Fio, there is something touching about her lack of cynicism. "The White Cliffs of Dover" also provided an important thematic inspiration for *Porco Rosso*: much like the episode's idealization of individual pioneering of technology demonstrated by the manner in which royal air-mail pilots tend and care for their own machines, the film also emphasizes the loving human touch of small airplane workshops, bursting with true creativity.

Animated works that previously inspired Miyazaki also strongly echo in *Porco Rosso*. The Fleischer brothers, who received an obvious homage in the abovementioned theatrical cartoon scene, also had a deeper influence on the film's slapstick scenes that are very reminiscent of the Fleischers' Popeye cartoons. Much like the absurd contests between Popeye and his rival Bluto over the affection of their love interest Olive Oil, the struggle between Marco and Curtis over the love of Gina (and later also Fio) begins as an aerial competition and ends with a violent fistfight. Even more notably, the design of the leader of the pirates' gang as an oversized buffoon also shows a strong influence of Bluto's character from the Fleischers' films. It is unclear if Miyazaki meant for this to be a direct reference, but as noted in Chapter 1 of this book, Bluto's character played an important role in the history of Japanese animation, "borrowed" without permission by Mitsuyo Seo for his World War II propaganda epics *Momotarō's Sea Eagle* and *Momotarō: Sacred Sailors*. In Seo's films, the character's stupidity and arrogance was meant to represent the Allies. *Porco Rosso*, of course, rejects the militant nationalism of the kind hailed by Seo's film, so the influence of the Fleischer brothers on the film has perhaps served Miyazaki as a means to comment on the historical roots of the very industry he is working in, beyond serving as mere inspiration for slapstick gags.

The Man Who Planted Trees was another important source of inspiration for *Porco Rosso*, particularly for a key scene in which, on the night before his big duel with Curtis, Marco tells Fio of a near-death

Miyazaki has balanced the grim, pessimistic political climate of the late 1920s with humorous touches inspired by the films of the Fleischer brothers and his own work on productions such as *Sherlock Hound*.

experience he had during the war. He recalls being hit during an aerial battle with German pilots, and waking up later in a sea of clouds, watching his dead comrades (as well as the enemy pilots) ascend to the heavens in their airplanes while he watches them helplessly. While telling the story, Marco's face briefly changes back to human form.

This scene strongly echoes Frederic Back's film, in the scenes portraying the first meeting between the old shepherd and the film's narrator. In a similar manner to the narrator who watches the old man counting the acorns he plans on planting the next day in front of candlelight, Fio watches Marco as he counts bullets he plans on using in the following day's battle in front of candlelight.[4] The following scene in Back's film has the shepherd recounting the tragic tale of losing his wife and son, leading to his decision to isolate himself from other people, much like Marco's tale of his own loss. As with other references, the scene in *Porco Rosso* shows respect for Back's film but does so with a twist. Like the old shepherd, Marco chose to "retire" from the human race following the trauma of loss. Yet unlike the protagonist of *The Man Who Planted Trees*, who is already overcoming the trauma by planting a forest and ensuring the future of his surroundings, Marco still relives his traumatic past: unlike the shepherd's acorns, the bullets he counts are instruments of death, not healing. Marco still needs to overcome his past, and he cannot possibly save the world that surrounds him, which still has a long way to go before healing.

Marco's flashback scene and his relationship with young Fio also refer to two of Miyazaki's important literary influences, both fittingly written by pilots who fought against fascism and concern flying. One is *They Shall Not Grow Old*, a short story by British author Roald Dahl (1916–1990). The story's unnamed narrator is a Royal Air Force pilot in The British Mandate of Palestine, flying missions against the forces of Vichy France in Lebanon. The story opens when Fin, a member of the narrator's squadron, fails to return from a mission and the other members assume that he was killed in action. Two days later, however, Fin reports back to the squadron with his plane—something that should be impossible, given the fuel limitation—and is unable to account for the lost time during which he was missing. Only after returning to fly with his comrades, Fin recalls what happened: he found himself enveloped by clouds, and saw a line of fighter planes ascending, realizing that these were the souls of dead pilots on their last journey—a clear inspiration for the scene described by Marco in the film.

Though better known for children's literary classics as *Charlie and the Chocolate Factory*, Dahl has also written many adult stories that were often quite dark; *They Shall Not Grow Old* originally appeared in the 1946 collection *Over to You: Ten Stories of Flyers and Flying*, which contained stories inspired by Dahl's service as a fighter pilot in World War II.[5] In *They Shall Not Grow Old* Dahl tells a story about people who are accompanied by death each day, going on each mission knowing that they might not come back and mourn for their fallen friends in a quiet and low-key manner, almost as if they've grown used to it. A sense of respect for the enemy's pilots is also felt throughout the story, as the protagonists realize that these pilots face the same fears and losses as well. The story provides the feeling that the thing which unites all fighter pilots, above all, is the sense of loss of their comrades and the story ends with Fin declaring "I'm a lucky bastard" just before he is about to die, knowing that he will soon join his friends (and foes) in the pilots' paradise that he caught a glimpse of. Marco's character in the film was not allowed into this paradise, and he must deal with the harsh Earthly realities, all while carrying the legacy of his dead comrades.

The second literary source that provided influence for *Porco Rosso* was Antoine de Saint-Exupéry's beloved book *The Little Prince*, originally published in 1943.[6] The book tells the story of the meeting between the narrator, a pilot whose airplane crashed in the Sahara Desert, and a strange little boy claiming to have come from a distant asteroid in space. While the narrator attempts to repair his airplane, the boy tells him of his voyages among different planets and the different people he met on each of them.

Saint-Exupéry was a daring French aviator who served with the pioneers of air-mail services while commercial flight was still in its infancy. He was also a gifted writer, whose books provided inspiration for countless pilots and flight enthusiasts, among them Miyazaki himself who praised Saint-Exupéry's memoir *Wind, Sand and Stars* (1939), which he first read at the age of 20. Miyazaki also spoke highly of Saint-Exupéry's beautiful illustrations throughout *The Little Prince*.[7] *The Little Prince* was written while France was under the occupation of Nazi Germany, and Saint-Exupéry was living in exile from his own homeland, serving as a pilot for the Allies. Though the exact circumstances surrounding his death are unclear, it is widely accepted that his plane was shot down during a reconnaissance mission over France.

Although classified as (and written in the style of) a children's book, *The Little Prince* is also a sophisticated allegory that makes a bitter commentary about the society and politics of its time. The characters described throughout the book, through the innocent eyes of the little boy who cannot understand the strange behavior of the adult world, represent less than flattering aspects of human behavior that are all too familiar for adult readers, such as greed, lust for power, and fame. The book carries a strong anti-fascist theme, and also reflects the author's deep resentment of his country's shameful surrender to tyranny.

Interestingly, though the politics of *Porco Rosso* are not very different from those of *The Little Prince*, the film makes no references to the book's sophisticated allegories or Saint-Exupéry's beautiful illustrations that accompany it. Instead, it draws most of its inspiration from the frame story—that of a daring pilot whose must repair a crashed plane, with the plane-crash serving as a metaphor for his emotional state, a sense of loss of direction. Like the pilot of Saint-Exupéry's book, Marco also regains his emotional strength through the friendship with a young character and its captivating, if naive, view of the complex adult world. While being primarily a story about an aging, bitter man, Fio's character serves as a reminder that young people and their optimistic view of the world can make things better—and this reminder serves as a strong thematic link between *Porco Rosso* and Miyazaki's previous works. His following film, however, moved further away from such optimism.

Released in 1997, *Princess Mononoke* (*Mononoke hime*) is a historical fantasy set during the Muromachi period (between the fourteenth and sixteenth centuries), a time of political instability and civil wars throughout Japan. The story opens with a small isolated village of the Emishi (a tribal group native to Japan, which in reality no longer existed as a separate social group during the time the film takes place) coming under attack by a giant mad boar. Ashitaka, the young tribe prince, kills the boar, but falls under the same curse that drove the boar mad—a curse that makes him almost invincible in battle, but also slowly fills him with hate and rage that will eventually bring his demise. In an attempt to remove the curse, Ashitaka chooses exile from his village, and goes on a journey westwards into the war-torn land. His journey brings him to Iron Town, a fortified city built and led by the ambitious Lady Eboshi who employs former prostitutes and other social outcasts in the service of her advanced firearms-manufacturing plant. It is here that Ashitaka discovers what led to his curse: the people of Iron Town have expanded their operation into the ancient forest, coming into a violent conflict with its animals and their mythical gods. The forest's forces are led by San, a young, hateful human girl raised by wolf-goddess Moro, whom the people of Iron Town refer to as "Princess Mononoke" ("Demon Princess"). Ashitaka, who falls in love with San, must find a way to bring peace to the two communities.

Almost 30 years after his work on *The Little Norse Prince*, Miyazaki told another story of a "civilized boy in the jungle"—Ashitaka, the protagonist of *Princess Mononoke*. But in this film, Miyazaki is obviously more pessimistic about the chances of such a boy to educate the people who surround him.

Princess Mononoke debuted in Japanese theatres in 1997, briefly topping the all-time Japanese box-office before losing this top spot to James Cameron's *Titanic*. This achievement testifies not only to the important place that Miyazaki's works came to employ in Japanese culture, but also of the manner in which the film itself refers to many elements common in these works in a critical manner, openly questioning their relevance in the face of changing times.

The film's concept originated over a decade before it even began production. In 1980, Miyazaki prepared a series of sketches aimed at interesting prospective production companies in an idea for a film about a love story between a mononoke monster and a young princess, his own take on the famous "Beauty and the Beast" legend set against a historical Japanese backdrop. No production company had shown interest in the proposal, and, before giving up on the project, Miyazaki published his sketches in a book accompanied by his initial story idea in 1983.[8]

Although the basic plot of Miyazaki's original proposal is very different from that of the 1997 film, key elements from it were retained: it contains a person (the princess' father) possessed by an evil spirit that makes him an invincible but also angry and ruthless warrior, the foundation of an iron industry that produces deadly weapons within a fortress, and the sense of a brutal war that ravages the land. The love story between the mononoke and the princess in the original proposal also echoes that of Ashitaka and San in the film—which is also the story of love between a human and a monster of sorts. The film, however, was far more complex in its presentation of each of its lover characters as a "monster"—the cursed Ashitaka is accepted by the human community (to a certain degree) while the human girl San is rejected by the same community as a "monster princess" simply for fighting on the other side.

The same complexity is also evident in the manner in which the original proposal and the film refer to Miyazaki's previous works. In the proposal, the Mononoke's attempts to force the princess into a marriage ceremony bring to mind the wedding sequences from both *The Castle of Cagliostro* and *Puss 'n Boots* inspired (in both cases) by Grimault's *The Shepherdess and the Chimney Sweep*. In Grimault's film, the disruption of the forced wedding symbolizes the end of tyranny and oppression; in the original proposal, the wedding ceremony is not disrupted (the princess simply refuses to go along with it until her father is saved, and the mononoke is finally convinced by her strong will—certainly an inspiration for the film's strong-willed character of San). In this manner,

Princess Mononoke, in both its original proposal and final film, is perhaps closer to *Panda and the Magic Serpent*—the film that inspired young Miyazaki to seek a career in animation, which also dealt with the love between a human and a creature considered as a monster, the social taboos that made this love forbidden, and implied of the greater tragedies that these taboos bring.

The original proposal does, however, portray the end of tyranny vividly: after the evil spirit who oppressed the people is defeated, the people burn down its fortress, including the iron plant in which they were enslaved. Iron Town is destroyed at the end of the film, but throughout it is not portrayed as a place of oppression or slavery; on the contrary, it is a place where social outcasts find honest work and make an honest living. The problem with Iron Town is not in how it treats its own people, but how in this treatment it harms the world that surrounds it. The idea that even the best political and social intentions can lead to negative results is far more complex than the utopian solutions to social problems rooted in Miyazaki's previous radical views, and expressed in his previous works.

Such utopian solutions often involved the ability of young people to shape their world, and *Princess Mononoke* is rather pessimistic about this possibility as well. Another early work by Miyazaki that can be discussed in this context is *Shuna's Journey* (*Shuna no Tabi*), a watercolor manga published in 1983.[9] The titular character is a young prince from an isolated valley whose people face a hard struggle against the dwindling of their crops. Upon hearing of the magical Golden Wheat that grows up in the distant Land of Gods, he embarks upon a journey to bring this wheat to his valley and save his people. His journey confronts him with the ugly side of humanity, as he encounters slavery, greed, and even cannibalism. But Shuna remains loyal to his moral principles, putting his own quest at risk when he rescues two sisters from a slave-trader, and is later repaid for his kindness.

Though by no means a sophisticated story, *Shuna's Journey* is beautifully drawn in a painterly style, bringing the journey of the title to life with nuances that give a different feeling to each location. It is also very much reflective of Miyazaki's previous works and sources of inspiration, as well as hinting of his future epics: the desert-like landscapes from *People of the Desert*, the elk-riding protagonist from Atamanov's *The Snow Queen*, as well as the wise old woman and the bandit leader from the same film, and the mysterious forbidden land populated with strange creatures reminiscent of both *Nausicaa of the Valley of the Wind* (both the manga, which began publication shortly before the appearance of *Shuna's Journey*, and the film, which came out a year later) and *Castle in the Sky*. The design of the two slave sisters in the manga is also reminiscent of both Nausicaa and Mei from *My Neighbor Totoro*.

The main significance of *Shuna's Journey*, however, is in setting the narrative frame for *Princess Mononoke*. While the original proposal discussed above contained many of the set pieces for the film, *Shuna's Journey* served as template for the film's plot. Much like the manga, *Princess Mononoke* is the story of an elk-riding prince from an isolated region, who travels to a distant land, witnessing the lows that humanity can sink into, eventually reaching the land of gods, literally (the forest in *Princess Mononoke* is home to the animal gods). As with other early works that echoed in Miyazaki's later career, this basic plot matured considerably by the time it was used in the film: Ashitaka's journey is not the journey of a prince on a quest to save his people—he leaves them knowing that they are doomed and that he will never come back.

The characters of both Shuna and Ashitaka draw their influence from a long line of male protagonists that have populated works directed by Miyazaki or involving him—from Ken of *Wolf Boy Ken*, to Hols and Conan: the civilized boy who educates the people of the jungle. But more than any previous production, *Princess Mononoke* emphasized how the social roles got reversed as the world got more modern: Ashitaka came from an ancient, peaceful culture, while the war-torn land he journeys to, supposedly more socially (and certainly technologically) "advanced" is every bit a violent "jungle." The animals of the forest descend from another peaceful and ancient culture, but they also adopt the modern way of warfare. Ashitaka's battle for peace, as the film shows, is a losing one. Even if the film's end implies hope, it is achieved at a tragic cost of many deaths. Other than Miyazaki's previous work that featured male protagonists, Ashitaka's journey appears to draw influence from the journey of the unnamed narrator in Back's *The Man Who Planted Trees*; upon his initial visit to the ravaged county, before meeting the shepherd, the narrator also meets many hostile and hateful people and comments on how making a living through coal-burning pollutes both the population's land and soul (another early inspiration, perhaps, for Iron Town). In both *Princess Mononoke* and Back's film, pollution and violence go hand in hand (the narrator's first visit to the county occurs shortly before the breakout of World War I), but *Princess Mononoke* is far more pessimistic about the chances of overcoming humanity's violent urges through the beauty of nature.

The female protagonists of *Princess Mononoke* also echo the strong, independent female characters seen in Miyazaki's previous works, especially *Nausicaa of the Valley of the Wind*. San, in particular, is the protector of nature in the mold of Nausicaa herself, who feels more comfortable in the company of the forest's dwellers than she does in the company of humankind. But her struggle to preserve the forest in the face of human development and violence is far more militant and violent in its own right, compared with Nausicaa's pacifism; her rebelliousness takes the social alienation of the characters that inspired Nausicaa—the Lady who Loved Insects and Homer's Phoenician princess—to far greater extremes. Additional inspiration for San's character came from Tera, a young girl who also lives in a community of outcasts, terrorizing the seemingly peaceful community of High Harbor in Miyazaki's earlier *Future Boy Conan*. Like San, Tera also wears a mask while conducting her nightly raids on High Harbor, exposing the faults in the ideal living of its people, and the limit of their tolerance. San is the cynical incarnation of Nausicaa, showing how the struggle for a good cause can easily deteriorate to violence—not unlike that seen in *Silent Running*.

On the other side is Lady Eboshi, the antagonist of *Princess Mononoke*, echoing Kushana of *Nausicaa of the Valley of the Wind*. Like Kushana, Eboshi is a ruthless military leader admired by her people, yet her militant approach is not portrayed in an entirely negative manner. In a ruthless world, Eboshi's ruthless leadership is effective in protecting the weak. This protection, of course, comes at a price, but it is clear that the admiration that the people of Iron Town feel toward their leader is not grounded only in her military might; she is also a compassionate woman who gave them means to support themselves and purpose to their lives—and in this respect, Eboshi is closer to Nausicaa than she is to Kushana. Like Nausicaa, Eboshi also keeps her own secret garden (another idea borrowed from *Silent Running*), showing that she has nothing against nature itself—her struggle against the gods of the forest is nothing but a territorial dispute.

And the Forest of the Gods, like Land of the Gods in *The Journey of Shuna*, the flying island of Laputa, and the places where Nausicaa is offered a chance to leave humanity behind is another forbidden paradise, a utopian place of natural beauty, devoid of the only element that could harm this perfection—human presence. In *The Journey of Shuna*, the inhabitants of this forbidden paradise take steps to ensure that their land will remain free of such presence, and do so violently, even though (and perhaps precisely because) this means mankind cannot enjoy the legendary Golden Wheat that grows in the land, meaning its extinction. In *Princess Mononoke*, the animal inhabitants of the forest of the gods take even more aggressive measures against the human population, declaring an all-out war (and the film's storming hordes of animals bring to mind both the animal gang of *Panda and the Magic Serpent* and even more noticeably the Halas and Batchelor adaptation of *Animal Farm*, which inspired it). Though Miyazaki rejects the forbidden paradise ideal, in *Princess Mononoke* he acknowledges that human presence indeed makes it—or any other kind of paradise—impossible, and the film ends on a doubtful note about the chances of productive human existence alongside nature. The film was Miyazaki's bitter farewell to the twentieth century.

Gazing into a Dark Future

In 1994, during the early stages of the production of *Princess Mononoke*, Miyazaki found time for a side-project when he was approached by Japanese pop-duo Chage and Aska to direct a music video for their song *On Your Mark*. The video takes place in a futuristic metropolis and opens with members of a paramilitary police unit raiding the headquarters of a mysterious cult. During the raid, two of the unit's members discover a young winged girl held captive by the cult—but it turns out that the unit's superiors have other plans for the angel girl, as they place her in a lab for further tests. The two officers who found the girl decide to rescue her again, this time from their own superiors.

Several stylistic elements in the video have the familiar Miyazaki feeling to them, especially in terms of character design: the two protagonists recall the pseudo-European look of Miyazaki's films (especially *Porco Rosso*), the angel girl's facial design is highly reminiscent of Nausicaa, and the lush, pastoral environment seen at both the beginning and the end of the video recalls the classic European scenery of *Heidi, Girl of the Alps*.

At the same time, with *On Your Mark* Miyazaki also stepped into a new territory of near-future science fiction. While *Nausicaa of the Valley of the Wind* took place in a post-apocalyptic society in which modern industry has vanished, and *Future Boy Conan* placed modern industry in a dystopian context where it is used to enslave people, *On Your Mark* takes place in a high-tech world of modern urban architecture, filled with skyscrapers and futuristic gadgets such as flying cars, possibly inspired by Jean Giraud's classic comic story *The Long Tomorrow*.[10] As such, *On Your Mark* is every bit a commentary on the negative social and environmental aspects of modern industrialization as Miyazaki's previous works—the modern city is seen in the video as a highly polluted and dangerous place—but also on the negative aspects of current and near-future technology, providing regimes and authorities with tools of oppression. The video does not even offer any kind of solution to the problems of the world seen in it—while the angel girl is saved at the end, she is merely released away from the polluted city, which (it can be assumed) continues to suffer from environmental and social problems.

In fact, this is just one ending of the video, and the more optimistic of the two. In directing *On Your Mark*, Miyazaki has presented his audience with two different conclusions, both included in it, and in the earlier pessimistic ending the two officers fail to save the girl and fall with her into a very deep abyss, presumably to their death. This indecisiveness regarding the manner in which the video should end shows an even deeper loss of way and direction than in Miyazaki's other films during the 1990s, and it echoes strongly in his twenty-first-century works.

The first of these works, *Spirited Away* (*Sen to Chihiro no Kamikakushi*) was Miyazaki's eighth feature-length animated film, and upon its release in 2001 made history when it surpassed *Princess Mononoke* in becoming the most successful all-time domestic film in Japan, later breaking the record held by *Titanic*, becoming Japan's all-time number one film at the box office.[11] An even more significant achievement might be the Academy Award given to the film in the Best Animated Feature category in 2003, bringing Miyazaki and his work to the attention of the public in North America; though by the time that *Spirited Away* won the award Miyazaki's work had been admired by American animators for over two decades, and despite the home-video release of *Kiki's Delivery Service* becoming a modest success, it was *Spirited Away* that made Miyazaki a household name among the American audience, which is somewhat surprising given the fact that it is hardly his most accessible or upbeat film.

Spirited Away begins in modern Japan, with a young girl named Chihiro moving to a new house with her parents. Chihiro is an introverted, frightened child who is highly dependent on the support of her parents, and is unhappy about the move to a new place or change in general. When her parents decide to take a detour on the way to their new house, they find themselves in a strange complex built in traditional Asian style. While Chihiro finds the place scary, her parents are enthralled by it, and soon get themselves into trouble when they eat freshly made food from a seemingly abandoned restaurant. The owner of the complex, an old witch named Yubaba, is very unhappy about her unwanted guests' behavior, and turns Chihiro's parents into pigs. With the help of a mysterious boy named Haku, Chihiro manages to avoid a similar fate and convince Yubaba to let her work in her bathhouse for gods, hoping to save her parents.

Spirited Away can be seen as the concluding chapter in a trilogy of Miyazaki films about growing up, which began with *My Neighbor Totoro* and continued with *Kiki's Delivery Service*; as in both previous films, there is a crisis that poses a threat to proper growth, a threat represented by the danger of losing one's immediate family. But while the threat of Mei and Satsuki losing their mother or that of Kiki's inability to live independently away from her family is based on the fear of losing loving and supporting parents, the crisis that Chihiro faces is much deeper. Chihiro's parents, as can be seen at the beginning of the film, neglect their child and treat her emotional dependence on them as a burden. Even in the final scene of the film, after the struggle against Yubaba, which made Chihiro a far stronger person both physically and emotionally, she still longs for an emotional support from her parents— and they still refuse to provide her with such support. In *Spirited Away*, Miyazaki has provided a grim view of the family in twenty-first-century Japan, with people so lost in their work to the point that they lose their

The slave-labor scenes of *Spirited Away*, Miyazaki's Academy Award-winning film, recall both the dystopian atmosphere of Grimault's *The Adventures of Mr. Wonderbird* and Miyazaki's own *Future Boy Conan*.

identity, and a growing unbridgeable gap between parents and their children—so different from the ideal manner in which he presented family life in his previous works.

Such a bitter correspondence with Miyazaki's previous works and works that inspired him continues all throughout *Spirited Away*. It is perhaps best evident in the way the film exposes the backstage in which hard and ungrateful work is done to keep the front, which the wide public sees, shiny and tempting—the traditional-looking beautiful street where Chihiro's parents get into trouble, as well as the well-organized bathhouse for gods are kept together by the staff of the bathhouse, which Yubaba employs under conditions that could almost be considered as slave-labor. This divide recalls both Grimault's *The Shepherdess and the Chimney Sweep* in which the evil king's beautiful yet eerily empty kingdom was supported by slave labor of the people who live underground, as well as Miyazaki's own *Future Boy Conan* in which the technological "utopia" of Industria kept functioning due to the work of slaves held in a similar manner. Both works ended, however, with the collapse of the corrupt regimes based on slavery, while Chihiro's victory over Yubaba is partial at best. Another strong parallel, in this respect, is to the scene in *Castle in the Sky* in which Pazu goes to help the old mechanic who operates the pirates' airship, discovering a fascinating world of machinery that makes the ship move. A similar scene in *Spirited Away* has Chihiro visiting the bathhouse's boiler room, where she meets its operator Kamaji (a character with a spider's body and a face very similar to that of the old mechanic in *Castle in the Sky*). Unlike Pazu's enthusiastic reaction to the new surroundings, Chihiro is frightened and awed by the sight of the mechanism, and the knowledge that she will become a part—and not a very significant one—of the bathhouse's inner works.

One recurring visual motif in *Spirited Away*, which also had a strong presence in its predecessor *Princess Mononoke*, is that of dirt and pollution—not just as an environmental issue but also as a metaphor for social and psychological greed. There is a strange paradox in the operation of Yubaba's bathhouse: on one hand, it is a place where strange creatures come to get clean, but on the other hand, Yubaba is clearly repelled by the sight of dirt—as is evident by her horrified reaction to a customer who arrives at the bathhouse buried under layers of filth (somewhat recalling the boar-god buried under layers of ugliness that represent his hate from the opening of *Princess Mononoke*). It is in this scene that Chihiro gets her chance to shine, helping the customer—who turns out to be a river-god—clean up and remove not only the filth that

covers him but also different objects that got stuck in his body (at this
point the scene makes a reference to a somewhat similar cleaning scene
in *Future Boy Conan*). While Yubaba is repelled by the sight of the dirty
god not just aesthetically but also in the deeper understanding that the
god's presence exposes the true ugly nature of her operation, Chihiro's
understanding of this nature and the injustice that is a part of it helps
her handle the situation. It is this scene in which the film starts showing
us a change in Chihiro: she gains confidence, and feels more prepared to
go on a quest to regain not only her parents but also her lost identity.

This quest for a lost identity was present in some of Miyazaki's
previous works. The people of Industria in *Future Boy Conan* were
subjected to a violent erasure of their past, and this treatment was
applied not only to the slave-laborers but also to the country's own
soldiers (one of the most emotional scenes in the show has Monsley
breaking down after having a flashback to her happy childhood) *The
Journey of Shuna* also had its protagonist dealing with the loss of his
memories as a punishment for stealing the wheat from the land of the
gods. This was not, however, a major theme in either work or in Miyazaki's
works in general, and its origins in *Spirited Away* can be traced to
Miyazaki's sources of inspiration.

One such source is *Night on the Milky Way Railway* (*Ginga Tetsudo no
Yoru*), a children's novel by Japanese poet Kenji Miyazawa (1896–1933).
As noted in Chapter 2, Miyazawa's novel was very much inspired by
Edmondo De Amicis' book *Cuore*, adapted into the World Masterpiece
Theatre show *3,000 Leagues in Search of Mother* on which Miyazaki
worked.[12]

Published in 1934 after its author's death, *Night on the Milky Way
Railway* is considered a masterpiece of Japanese literature. The story
follows Giovanni, a young boy who must work to take care of his sick
mother in the absence of his father, and who suffers constant mocking
from his classmates about the hard life he leads. One night, on his way
home back from work, Giovanni boards a mysterious train that takes
him on a journey through the night's sky. As the journey progresses,
Giovanni realizes that the other passengers on the train—including his
friend Campanella—are the souls of dead children on their way to the
afterlife. Upon waking up, and realizing that his friend has indeed died
while saving another boy from drowning, the grief-stricken Giovanni
vows to remain strong in face of the hardships of life.

Night on the Milky Way Railway reflects many of Miyazawa's beliefs,
rooted in his Buddhist faith about the need to help others (Miyazawa

himself devoted much of his life to helping poor farmers in Japan). A key scene in *Spirited Away* has Chihiro—now hardened by the experience of working in the bathhouse—declaring an open rebellion against Yubaba, leaving the bathhouse to save Haku. She travels to get help on a strange train that, much like the one boarded by Giovanni, carries many passengers with a ghostly appearance. Much like the journey that Giovanni went through, Chihiro's journey convinces her to hang on to life, to purpose, regardless of the difficulties she encounters.

Other literary works, as well as their cinematic adaptations, may have inspired Chihiro's quest for identity, notably a short sequence from Atamanov's *The Snow Queen* in which the heroine had to struggle against an attempt to make her forget her identity and mission. An even stronger source of influence may be *The Last Unicorn*, the 1982 adaptation of Peter S. Beagle's acclaimed fantasy novel. As noted in Chapter 4, the film was directed by Jules Bass and Arthur Rankin and animated by the Topcraft studio, which worked on Miyazaki's *Nausicaa of the Valley of the Wind*.

The Last Unicorn follows a unicorn that goes on a search for others of her kind, encountering many examples of human greed and selfishness along her journey. At one point she is captured by an old witch who uses her as part of her freak circus of magical animals; the circus display, much like Yubaba's bathhouse, "robs" the magical animals presented in it of their true identity by applying them with ugly prosthetics that are meant to give them a more "magical" appearance while hiding their true nature. The unicorn is helped by the witch's young apprentice who—much like Haku—got caught in the witch's service following his naive ambitions to become a great wizard. The cage in which the unicorn is imprisoned is even locked by a padlock that changes into the witch's face, recalling the doorknobs with faces that lead to Yubaba's office in *Spirited Away*.

Another significant struggle for identity takes place at a later part of the film, in which the unicorn is turned into a human, and must fight to keep memories of her former existence while trapped in the castle of a hostile king. Regaining the unicorn's true identity involves a feat of courage and her love for a man who came to her aid, not unlike Chihiro's path to regaining her identity.

Spirited Away deserves the accolades it received and despite its complex structure was a proper introduction to Miyazaki's works for large audiences outside Japan; despite reflecting the confusion and chaos of the early twenty-first century, it is a carefully constructed film with many visual wonders and a strong emotional core. Miyazaki's two subsequent films retained the emotional core, but had difficulty balancing the new century's confusion with a strong narrative backbone.

The first of these two films, *Howl's Moving Castle* (2004), was based on a book by renowned British children's author Diana Wynne Jones.[13] It tells the story of Sophie, a talented but unconfident hatter, who draws the attention of the young beautiful wizard, Howl. The evil witch of the waste, jealous of Howl's feelings toward Sophie, curses Sophie and turns her into an old woman, robbing her not only of her youth but also of the ability to tell anyone of her true condition. Sophie seeks help in the wastelands, finding refuge in Howl's own enormous moving castle, befriending the wizard's young assistant Markl, the castle's fire-demon Calcifer, and a mysterious moving scarecrow in an attempt to remove the curse she is under. But greater things are at work: the country is in the middle of a deadly war into which the royal family wishes to recruit Howl, and there is a mystery surrounding the identity of Howl himself.

Like *Spirited Away* before it, *Howl's Moving Castle* is a visual feast. In the tradition of *Castle in the Sky* and *Kiki's Delivery Service*, it features beautiful pseudo-European background art and imaginative fantasy flying machines, this time with a strong French inspiration: the design of the film's locations was inspired by the Alsace region while its fantasy-technology designs were inspired by nineteenth-century French cartoonist Albert Robida, whose work was highly influential on early Japanese science fiction.[14] The choice of a French feeling for the film's design, despite the English background of Wynne Jones' original novel, is perhaps rooted in the fact that Miyazaki's previous film *Castle in the Sky* was set in a pseudo-British environment.

Howl's Moving Castle also recalls *Spirited Away* in the relationship between its two protagonists—the relationship between Sophie and Howl is strongly reminiscent of that between Chihiro and Haku, with the love of the two characters able to save the mysterious boy who keeps a dark secret. In the film, this secret manifests in the form of the castle—an ugly, messed-up structure that sometimes seems to be a deliberate caricature of the evil king's castle of Grimault's *The Shepherdess and the Chimney Sweep* (another French source of inspiration for the film), representing the childish side of each castle owner and Although Howl is far from the selfishness and greed that characterized the evil king, the childhood fantasy he lives in proves to be equally destructive; after modeling villain characters such as Count Cagliostro and Muska in the mold of the evil king, in *Howl's Moving Castle* Miyazaki argues that such a character is also a victim of its own behavior. *Howl's Moving Castle* ends with the destruction of the castle (also modeled on the end of Grimault's film, an ending referenced by Miyazaki in his previous works)—representing the end of childhood, and the need to move on to adult life. This need was also the theme behind works such as *My Neighbor Totoro* and *Kiki's Delivery Service*, but in *Howl's Moving Castle* it is expressed with a measure of brutality.

This theme is also expressed through Sophie's character—a young girl who finds herself trapped in the body of the "wise old woman" character, familiar from Miyazaki's previous works. Though Sophie does not possess the many years of life experience that were typical of these female characters in Miyazaki's other works, she is quick to discover that in her new identity, while physically limited, she is a far more confident person, and that old age has its advantages. While Howl is the childish man who cannot grow up, Sophie plays the film's responsible adult—a role forced on her, but one that she grows used to, and one in which she eventually saves the day.

But against the strength of its characters, *Howl's Moving Castle* has a problem maintaining a balanced plot. The film changes direction too often, with several elements—notably the raging war—not feeling as an integral part of the whole. While unexpected plot twists and turns were also characteristic of *Spirited Away*, in *Howl's Moving Castle* there is the feeling that Miyazaki has at some point lost control of the film.

If *Howl's Moving Castle* felt like a film with too many plots and subplots, Miyazaki's next film suffers from the opposite problem: it feels somewhat uneventful, despite its attempts to impress the audience with grand visions of the forces of nature. Released in 2008, *Ponyo* follows a young princess of the underwater kingdom, who decides to leave her house and go living in the human kingdom, having befriended a human boy named Sosuke. But this decision greatly disturbs the natural order, resulting in a tsunami that hits the harbor-town Sosuke lives in. Can the love of Ponyo and Sosuke overcome nature itself?

After almost two decades of films with darker themes, *Ponyo* attempts to return to the earlier optimism of *My Neighbor Totoro* and *Kiki's Delivery Service*. *Castle in the Sky* is also echoed in *Ponyo* in its story of two children who go on a grand adventure to save the world. But Miyazaki's earlier films relied quite heavily on nostalgia, a longing for childhood. *Ponyo* attempts to paint an ideal childhood in a contemporary twenty-first-century setting, one that is full of environmental problems and natural disasters, and the end result has an odd feeling to it—like an attempt to bring together the abovementioned optimism into the grim apocalypse of *Nausicaa of the Valley of the Wind*. This connection between these two elements feels forced and unnatural, and at times it is unclear if the tsunami scenes in the film are meant to evoke fear or amusement.

Ponyo also feels inferior to Miyazaki's previous optimistic films on another level: it is a film in which childhood fantasies triumph over adult realities. *My Neighbor Totoro* and *Kiki's Delivery Service* both emphasized the power of childhood fantasies to overcome the difficulties of reality but, in both films, these fantasies were means rather than ends; they served as a tool on the path to a successful adulthood, and did not represent childhood as something that people should remain in forever. *Ponyo* does the opposite: both Sosuke and Ponyo insist on maintaining their friendship, forcing the adult society around them to accept it. Neither character grows or develops, as opposed to the emotional journey of Mei, Satsuki, and Kiki. The decision to focus the film over an external conflict— against the forces of nature—rather than an internal one, against a family crisis or the lack of confidence, makes *Ponyo* less thematically interesting. The insistence of both protagonists on their innocent love for one another, despite social taboos, also recalls *Panda and the Magic Serpent*—the film that initially inspired Miyazaki to choose a career in animation (Chihiro and Haku's relationship, as well as Sophie and Howl's, also recalls the impossible love story from this film, though to a lesser extent). But *Panda and the Magic Serpent* emphasized the many hardships involved in overcoming this taboo; there are virtually no hardships in *Ponyo*.

As with *Howl's Moving Castle* before it, *Ponyo* makes up for its narrative shortcomings with its visual strength. The direction chosen for the film is somewhat less detailed compared with previous efforts, giving it a feeling of an illustrated children's book rather than a highly detailed fantasy world. But characters remain expressive and well-animated as always, from Ponyo's hyperactive curiosity (somewhat recalling the charming scenes of Mei from *My Neighbor Totoro*) through the clumsiness of Ponyo's father to the determination of Sosuke's mother, making *Ponyo* an entertaining film, if not a very deep one.

The Boy Who Dreamed of Airplanes

As the first decade of the twenty-first century gave way to the second, Miyazaki began work on what he would announce to be his final feature-length film—an animated biopic about Jirō Horikoshi, the designer of the legendary Zero fighter planes used by the Japanese army during World War II. Horikoshi's true story was combined with the 1937 fictional story *Kaze Tachinu* (*The Wind Rises*), which also gave the film its title, by Japanese writer Tatsuo Hori. Hori's story followed a woman hospitalized in a sanitarium for tuberculosis patients; in Miyazaki's film, this character became Horikoshi's great love, a woman named Naoko. The film follows the rise of Horikoshi in the Japanese aviation industry parallel to his doomed affair with Naoko, whose condition keeps getting worse.

The Wind Rises weaves together elements from Miyazaki's own biography and filmography; at times the movie seems full of ghosts from the director's past. The story of Naoko's struggle with her disease echoes Miyazaki's mother's own struggle with tuberculosis, while Horikoshi's own story of a boy who dreams of airplanes and grows up to become a great artist, inspiring those around him, is very much the story of Miyazaki himself, who grew up admiring the airplanes that were handled by his family's factory, and became a leading animator inspiring those who work with him and those who practice animation all over the world.

But historical context cannot be ignored. Horikoshi designs his planes and pushes Japanese aviation forward at a time when Japan is getting more and more militant, and his masterpieces will eventually serve the country in a murderous war. In the course of the film Horikoshi meets with one of his heroes, legendary German plane designer Hugo Junkers, and later learns that Junkers became a political enemy of his own country when the Nazis came to power. Horikoshi himself comes under the suspicion of the Japanese secret police as the film progresses, and yet he keeps designing airplanes that will eventually become tools in the hands of the Japanese army; he keeps chasing the dreams of aircraft design and his love for Naoko, knowing full-well that the realization of both dreams will end tragically.

The realization of both dreams is full of references to the past works of Miyazaki and his colleagues. The film's opening sequence alone, showing Horikoshi as a young boy who dreams of meeting and flying with Italian aircraft designer Giovanni Caproni, brings to mind so many of these works—from the dream-flight sequence of Yoshifumi Kondō's *Little Nemo: Adventures in Slumberland* pilot film, through the moonlight flight sequence of Satsuki and Mei in *My Neighbor Totoro* to the early scenes of planes filled with children in *Porco Rosso* (in which several featured airplanes were inspired by real-life aircraft designed by Caproni's company).

These references to the portrayals of happy childhood are followed by references to the portrayals of darker times: when Horikoshi visits Germany, he witnesses how a scared man is being chased by a gang of bullies—perhaps a Nazi gang terrorizing civilians (even though the scene takes place before the Nazi party came to power). This portrayal of Germany as a dark and grim place reflects not only history, but also the suffocating and threatening urban design of Frankfurt in *Heidi, Girl of the Alps*. The audience is reminded of the political situation in Germany in a later scene featuring a German refugee in Japan named Castorp who informs Horikoshi about Junker's fall out of favor in German with the rise of the Nazi regime. When Castorp is quick to identify Horikoshi, the amazed young airplane designer asks if the German is somehow related to Sherlock Holmes—an amusing reference to Miyazaki's own work on *Sherlock Hound*.

Castorp's character is itself a reference to another work: the 1924 literary masterpiece *The Magic Mountain* by German author Thomas Mann.[15] In Mann's novel, a man named Castorp visits his cousin who is recovering from tuberculosis in a sanatorium in the Alps. The visit becomes an existential experience during which Castorp falls in love and engages in deep intellectual discussions with other characters that represent different aspects of humanity in the early twentieth century. But the true nature of humanity is revealed when Castorp is forced to leave the sanatorium and fight in World War I, a time of violent barbarism. Much like Mann's character, Castorp meets Horikoshi and discusses world affairs with him in a pastoral resort, away from the world's troubles, the perfect backdrop for Horikoshi's and Naoko's first meeting. Castorp helps the love between the two bloom, accompanying it with his piano-playing of the romantic German song *Das gibt's nur einmal* (*It Only Happened Once*) for them. This song is a reference to another work, taken from the popular 1931 German musical film *Der Kongress tanzt* about the 1814 Congress of Vienna, which was aimed at establishing peaceful world order. Alas, reality cannot be ignored: Naoko is fighting a losing battle with her disease, Castorp (like Mann himself, and most of the team that worked on *Der Kongress tanzt*) is a man who got banished from his own country.

And so the film ends, on a grim note. Following Naoko's death, Horikoshi dreams again of Caproni who shows him his handiwork—if Horikoshi's planes made a difference, it was only for the worse. The final scene in the film has Horikoshi watching his planes used as death tools in the service of war, his work made a mockery. It is a tragic, and even chilling, view of Miyazaki's reflection of his own work.

And yet, despite his announcement about retiring from feature filmmaking after *The Wind Rises*, Miyazaki appears to have found enough inspiration, and perhaps even hope, in the twenty-first century as well. At the time of this writing, he is working on a new feature film.

Notes

1   McCarthy, *Hayao Miyazaki, Master of Japanese Animation*, 140–143.
2   For a discussion of the series, see Daniel Thomas, "Miyazaki Comics—The Age of the Flying Boat (1989)," Ghibli Blog (2010). Available online: http:// ghiblicon.blogspot.co.il/2010/03/miyazaki-comics-age-of-flying-boat-1989.html
3   McCarthy, *Hayao Miyazaki, Master of Japanese Animation*, 160–164.
4   Special thanks to Steven Ng for pointing out this parallel in a message to the Hayao Miyazaki Discussion Group mailing list on October 12, 2000.
5   Roald Dahl, *Over to You: Ten Stories of Flyers and Flying* (London: Penguin Books, 1973), 113–130. On a related note, Miyazaki has expressed his admiration for Dahl's autobiographical writing in *Turning Point*, 154–155.
6   Antoine de Saint-Exupéry, *The Little Prince* (London: Bibliophile Books, 1995).
7   Hayao Miyazaki, *Turning Point*, 176–183; 406–409. Miyazaki has expressed his particular appreciation for Saint-Exupéry's descriptions of his ordeals as air-mail delivery pilot in the early days of aviation; this appreciation may have found its way to "The White Cliffs of Dover" as well.
8   Hayao Miyazaki, *Princess Mononoke: The First Story* (San Francisco: Viz Media, 2014).
9   Hayao Miyazaki, *Shuna no Tabi* (Tokyo: Tokuma Shoten, 1983).
10 Jean Giraud, *Moebius 4: The Long Tomorrow and Other Science Fiction Stories* (New York: The Marvel Entertainment Group, 1987).
11 Andrew Osmond, *Spirited Away* (London: British Film Institute, 2008), 7–8.
12 See Osmond, *Spirited Away* for further discussion (15–19).
13 Diana Wynne Jones, *Howl's Moving Castle* (New York: HarperCollins, 2001).
14 Philippe Williams, *The 20th Century, Albert Robida: Translation, Introduction & Critical Material* (Middletown: Wesleyan University Press, 2004).
15 Thomas Mann, *The Magic Mountain* (New York: Alfred A. Knopf, 1995).

A GUIDE TO FURTHER RESEARCH

There are two major categories of books in English that examine Miyazaki's works: one consists of books that examine these works in the context of a larger study of anime or Japanese popular culture, and the other consists of fewer books that are devoted to Miyazaki exclusively. You will find more books from the first category referred to in the chapters of this book; this is not because books from the second category are not good, but rather because they focus on a creative period different from the one examined throughout most of this book—Miyazaki's career as a feature-film director, rather than his early days as an animator. This chapter offers a brief review of recommended books from both categories, not necessarily related to the theme of this book, but providing a good starting point for any research about the director and his works.

Books about Miyazaki

Daisuke Akimono, "War and Peace" in Studio Ghibli Films: Director Hayao Miyazaki's Messages for World Peace *(Saarbucken: Lambert Academic Publishing, 2014)*

This book offers a political reading of Studio Ghibli's films, focusing on Miyazaki's features. Author Akimono, a professor at the Soka University Peace Research Institute, demonstrates how the political themes of Miyazaki's films have evolved throughout the years in accordance with the shift in global politics, from the cold war to the war on terror. The stiff structure, which reads a bit too much like a thesis manuscript, can make reading a bit challenging, but Akimono's analysis is well worth the effort.

Helen McCarthy, Hayao Miyazaki: Master of Japanese Animation: Films, Themes, Artistry *(Berkeley: Stone Bridge Press, 1999)*

The first-ever book in the English language devoted entirely to Miyazaki and his films. Published at a time when most of his works were still unavailable for the audience in the English-speaking world, the book served as an introduction to the director for many readers and scholars. Opening with a biography of Miyazaki, the book follows with seven chapters, each covering another feature directed by him (from *The Castle of Cagliostro* to *Princess Mononoke*), providing information on production, a detailed synopsis, and an analysis of the film's themes. It's an accessible, passionately written work by an admitted fan of the director and his works that nonetheless provides many in-depth conclusions. Sadly, an updated edition that covers Miyazaki's twenty-first-century work is yet to appear.

Hayao Miyazaki, Nausicaa of the Valley of the Wind: Watercolor Impressions *(San Francisco: Viz Media, 2007)*

Viz Media has published art books for all of Miyazaki's films (and several non-Miyazaki Ghibli films as well), but this volume transcends the regular format of other books in the series, exploring the deeper roots of both the *Nausicaa of the Valley of the Winds* original manga and film adaptation, discussing original proposals, drafts, sketches, and the sources of inspiration for Miyazaki's magnum-opus.

Hayao Miyazaki, Starting Point: 1979–1996 *(San Francisco: Viz Media, 2009)*

Hayao Miyazaki, Turning Point: 1997–2008 *(San Francisco: Viz Media, 2014)*

These two volumes offer a deep look into Miyazaki's thoughts on a variety of subjects, mostly focusing on animation but also often wandering into the territory of political and social commentary. Fans and scholars of Miyazaki's films will find a wealth of information here in the form of many different production documents and reviews written by Miyazaki himself, along with lengthy interviews conducted with him throughout his career. The production documents and reviews are the most accessible materials in the two volumes whereas the interviews tend to be somewhat repetitive and can sometimes be a chore to work through; the first volume, covering the first part of Miyazaki's career from 1979 to 1996, contains mostly the first kind of content while the second volume, covering Miyazaki's career from 1997 to 2008, contains mostly the second kind.

Andrew Osmond, Spirited Away *(New York: Palgrave Macmillan, 2008)*

This slim book, published as part of the British Film Institute's series on film and television classics, packs an impressive amount of insights on Miyazaki's Academy Award-winning film, exploring its themes, stylistic choices, and their cultural meanings, and most importantly in the context of the book you are currently reading—Miyazaki's career, going as far back as his early days at Tōei to trace the roots of *Spirited Away's* success.

Eric Reinders, The Moral Narratives of Hayao Miyazaki *(Jefferson: McFarland & Company, 2016)*

This book offers a study of the moral perception expressed by Miyazaki's films through the analysis of religious elements in his films, covering all the films that he has directed except *The Castle of Cagliostro.* The book is very contradictive in terms of quality: while offering a rich analysis based on themes from Christianity, Buddhism, Shinto, Greek mythology, and even J.R.R. Tolkien's *Lord of the Rings* trilogy, Reinders strangely insists on ignoring the production context of the films he analyzes, and seems to be embarrassed by their classification as anime. Coupled with a sometimes overtly personal tone that's a little hard to take seriously, *The Moral Narratives of Hayao Miyazaki* is an interesting but flawed book.

Books that Discuss Miyazaki

Jonathan Clements, Anime: A History *(New York: Palgrave Macmillan, 2013)*

The definitive book on the history of Japanese animation, Clements' research details the rise of the anime industry as we know it, from the independent animators of the early twentieth century to the foundation of the post-war anime studios, showing how key productions have responded to the rise of new technologies starting with cinema, followed by television and video and the digital age. Miyazaki and his films are discussed extensively in the book, and rich background on the different studios and production companies that employed him is provided.

Susan Napier, Anime from Akira to Howl's Moving Castle *(New York: Palgrave Macmillan, 2005)*

Offering an analysis of different elements in Japanese culture through a variety of examples from popular anime works, Napier devotes two chapters in her book to a discussion of Miyazaki: one examines female characters in his films, their uniqueness in comparison with other anime heroines and their reflection of the director's nostalgia to a past that may have never existed; another analyzes the concept of femininity through the historical aspect of *Princess Mononoke*. Although not referring to the production background or Miyazaki's earlier career, the analysis in both chapters is deep and thought-provoking, and its conclusions easily apply to the works discussed in this book as well.

Alistair Swale, Anime Aesthetics: Japanese Animation and the "Post-Cinematic" Imagination *(New York: Palgrave Macmillan, 2015)*

What makes animation so different from any other form of cinema, and what makes anime in particular so different in its own right? Swale attempts to answer this question by examining case-studies of popular anime works from different perspectives. Miyazaki's work is often referred to as part of a larger discussion in Swale's book rather than on its own merits, but his observations—notably on the tension between Miyazaki's attempts to entertain and his wish to deliver a serious commentary—are sharp and thoughtful.

Jack Zipes, The Enchanted Screen: The Unknown History of Fairy-Tale Films *(New York: Routledge, 2011)*

In this book, fairy-tale scholar Jack Zipes offers a highly critical examination of the genre in its cinematic form, including a discussion of *Spirited Away* that also refers to Miyazaki's early career. The high-brow style may be off-putting to some readers—at times, the book gives the impression that Zipes is dismissive toward Hollywood genre films simply because they are Hollywood (and praises non-Hollywood films—such as Miyazaki's—because they're not), but the book is well worth reading, not just for Zipes' commentary on Miyazaki but also for his commentary on his sources of inspiration, as he discusses the Fleischer brothers and Paul Grimault as well.

Online Sources

Nausicaa.net (http://www.nausicaa.net/wiki/Main_Page)

This online database, maintained by Miyazaki and Studio Ghibli fans since 1996, and converted to a Wiki format in 2008, offers extensive information on Studio Ghibli—films, people, and related issues such as merchandise. Information on pre-Ghibli productions involving Miyazaki and Takahata is also available through the site, alongside translations of interviews and scripts, although it is not as easily accessible and requires some digging in comparison with the readily-available information on the studio's films.

Ghibli Blog (http://ghiblicon.blogspot.co.il/)

Although more a fan website than a database, this blog, maintained by Daniel Thomas, features many posts that examine Studio Ghibli's works, along with discussion of the studio's films, as well as projects helmed by the studio's figureheads before the studio's foundation. It is an excellent source of information and discussion about pre-Ghibli productions involving Miyazaki, although reaching relevant posts on the subject takes some searching through the blog's archives.

Lupin III: Castle of Cagliostro Commentary Track (https://terrania. us/2017/06/15/cagliostro-redux/)

This project by online critic and blogger Chris Meadows started in 2004, when he recorded a commentary track that provides insights and explores details and themes throughout Miyazaki's first feature-length film as a director. It has since been updated several times, with references to the ongoing influence of the film on subsequent productions. Meadows' analysis of every scene and his attention to small details makes repeated viewing of the film highly rewarding.

BIBLIOGRAPHY

AbdelRahim, Layla. *Children's Literature, Domestication and Social Foundation: Narratives of Civilization and Wilderness*. New York: Routledge, 2015.

Akamatsu, Yoshiko. "Japanese Readings of Anne of Green Gables," in *L.M. Montgomery and Canadian Culture*, edited by Irene Gammel and Elizabeth Epperly, 201–212. Toronto: University of Toronto Press, 1999.

Akimono, Daisuke. *"War and Peace" in Studio Ghibli Films: Director Hayao Miyazaki's Messages for World Peace*. Saarbucken: Lambert Academic Publishing, 2014.

Aldiss, Brian. *Hothouse*. London: Penguin Classics, 2008.

"A Talk between Hayao Miyazaki and Moebius," *Nausicaa.net* (2005). Available online: http://www.nausicaa.net/miyazaki/interviews/miyazaki_moebious.html

Baudou, Jacques. "Lupin, Arsene," in *The Oxford Companion to Crime and Mystery Writing*, edited by Rosemary Herbert, Catherine Aird, John M. Reilly, and Susan Oleksiw, 273. Oxford: Oxford University Press, 1999.

Beck, Jerry. *The Animated Movie Guide*. Chicago: A Cappella Books, 2005.

Bengal, Kate. "Theft," in *The Oxford Companion to Crime and Mystery Writing*, edited by Rosemary Herbert, Catherine Aird, John M. Reilly, and Susan Oleksiw, 456–457. Oxford: Oxford University Press, 1999.

Binson, T.J. "Gentleman Thief," in *The Oxford Companion to Crime and Mystery Writing*, edited by Rosemary Herbert, Catherine Aird, John M. Reilly, and Susan Oleksiw, 180. Oxford: Oxford University Press, 1999.

Brennan, Kristen. "Other Science Fiction." *Star Wars Origins* (2006). Available online: http://moongadget.com/origins/droids.html

Brennan, Kristen. "The Droids." *Star Wars Origins* (2006). Available online: http://moongadget.com/origins/droids.html

Brubaker, Charles. "The Animated History of 'Moomin'." *Cartoon Research* (2014). Available online: http://cartoonresearch.com/index.php/the-troubles-of-moomin/

Chapman, David and Gori, Gigliola. "Strong, Athletic and Beautiful: Edmondo De Amicis and the Ideal Italian Woman." *The International Journal of the History of Sport* 27, 11 (2010): 1968–1967.

Chiba, Tetsuya. *Chiba Testuya Official Site* (2004). Available online: http://chibapro.co.jp/en_index.php

Clements, Jonathan. *Schoolgirl Milky Crisis: Adventures in the Anime and Manga Trade*. London: Titan Books, 2010.

Clements, Jonathan. *Anime: A History*. London: BFI, 2013.

Clements, Jonathan and McCarthy, Helen. *The Anime Encyclopedia, 3rd Revised Edition*. Berkeley: Stone Bridge Press, 2015.

Corben, Richard. *Rowlf/Underground 3*. New York: Catalan Communications, 1987.

"Creation of the Taarna Sequence," *Celebrating Taarna* (2002). Available online: http://www.taarna.net/history.html

Dahl, Roald. *Over to You: Ten Stories of Flyers and Flying*. London: Penguin Books, 1973.

De Amicis, Edmondo. *Cuore (Heart): An Italian Schoolboy's Journal*. New York: Thomas Y. Crowell Company, 1915.

Evslin, Bernard. *Gods, Demigods and Demons: An Encyclopedia of Greek Mythology*. New York: Scholastic Book Services, 1975.

Fukushima, Tetsuji. *Sabaku no Mao 2*. Tokyo: Akita Shoten, 2012.

Gan, Sheuo-Hui. "To Be or Not to Be: The Controversy in Japan over the 'Anime' Label." *Animation Studies* (2009). Available online: http://journal. animationstudies.org/sheuo-hui-gan-to-be-or-not-to-be-anime-the-controversy-in-japan-over-the-anime-label/

Grant, John. *Masters of Animation*. New York: Watson-Guptill Publications, 2001.

Giraud, Jean. *Moebius 2: Arzach and Other Fantasy Stories*. New York: The Marvel Entertainment Group, 1987.

Giraud, Jean. *Moebius 4: The Long Tomorrow and Other Science Fiction Stories*. New York: The Marvel Entertainment Group, 1987.

Greenberg, Raz. "An Auteur is Born: 30 Years of Hayao Miyazaki's Castle of Cagliostro," *Animated Views* (2009). Available online: http:// animatedviews.com/2009/an-auteur-is-born-30-years-of-miyazakis-castle-of-cagliostro/

Greenberg, Raz. "The Illustrated Man," *Salon Futura* (2011). Available online: http://www.salonfutura.net/2011/02/the-illustrated-man/

Greenberg, Raz. "Giri and Ninjo: The Roots of Hayao Miyazaki's 'My Neighbor Totoro' in Animated Adaptations of Classic Children's Literature." *Literature Film Quarterly* 40, 2 (2012): 96–108.

Griswold, Jerry. *Feeling Like a Kid: Childhood and Children's Literature*. Baltimore: The Johns Hopkins University Press, 2006.

"Hayao Miyazaki," *Anime News Network* (2017). Available online: http://www. animenewsnetwork.com/encyclopedia/people.php?id=51

"Hayao Miyazaki and Isao Takahata Filmography," *Nausicaa.net* (2004). Available online: http://www.nausicaa.net/miyazaki/films/filmography. html

Herbert, Brian and Anderson, Kevin J. *The Road to Dune*. New York: Tor Books, 2005.

Herbert, Frank. *Dune*. New York: Ace Books, 2010.

Herman, Robert. *This Borrowed Earth: Lessons from the Fifteen Worst Environmental Disasters Around the World*. New York: Palgrave Macmillan, 2010.

Ikeda, Hiroshi. "The Background of Making of Flying Phantom Ship," in *Japanese Animation: East Asian Perspectives* edited by Masao Yokota and Tze-yue G. Hu, 287–296. Jackson: University of Mississippi Press, 2014.

Kano, Seiji. *Nippon no Animation o Kizuita Hitobito*. Tokyo: Wakakusa Shobo, 2004.

Kelly, George. "Caper," in *The Oxford Companion to Crime and Mystery Writing*, edited by Rosemary Herbert, Catherine Aird, John M. Reilly, and Susan Oleksiw, 55–56. Oxford: Oxford University Press, 1999.

Kermode, Mark. *Silent Running*. London: BFI, 2014.

Key, Alexander. *The Incredible Tide*. New York: Open Road, 2014.

Mann, Thomas. *The Magic Mountain*. New York: Alfred A. Knopf, 1995.

McCarthy, Helen. *Hayao Miyazaki, Master of Japanese Animation: Films, Themes, Artistry*. Berkeley: Stone Bridge Press, 1999.

McCarthy, Helen. *The Art of Osamu Tezuka, God of Manga*. New York: Abrams Comic Arts, 2009.

Miyao, Daisuke. "Before Anime: Animation and the Pure Film Movement in pre-war Japan." *Japan Forum* 14, 2 (2002): 191–209.

Miyazaki, Hayao. *Shuna no Tabi*. Tokyo: Tokuma Shoten, 1983.

Miyazaki, Hayao. *The Art of My Neighbor Totoro*. San Francisco: Viz Media, 2005.

Miyazaki, Hayao. *The Art of Kiki's Delivery Service*. San Francisco: Viz Media, 2006.

Miyazaki, Hayao. *The Art of Nausicaa of the Valley of the Wind, Watercolor Impressions*. San Francisco: Viz Media, 2007.

Miyazaki, Hayao. *Starting Point: 1979–1996*. San Francisco: Viz Media, 2009.

Miyazaki, Hayao. *Turning Point: 1997–2008*. San Francisco: Viz Media, 2014.

Miyazaki, Hayao. *Princess Mononoke: The First Story*. San Francisco: Viz Media, 2014.

Monkey Punch, *Lupin III Vol. 1*. Los Angeles: Tokyopop, 2002.

Moore, Robert. "Introduction: Why Cast a Spotlight on Joss Whedon?" in *Joss Whedon: The Complete Companion*, edited by Mary Alice Money, 19–21. London, Titan Books, 2012.

Napier, Susan. "Vampires, Psychic Girls, Flying Women and Sailor Scouts: Four faces of the young female in Japanese Popular Culture," in *The Worlds of Japanese Popular Culture*, edited by Dolores P. Martinez, 91–109. Cambridge: Cambridge University Press, 1998.

Napier, Susan. *Anime from Akira to Howl's Moving Castle*. New York: Palgrave Macmillan, 2005.

Nikolajeva, Maria. "A Misunderstood Tragedy: Astrid Lindgren's 'Pippi Longstocking' Books," in *Beyond Babar: The European Tradition in*

Children's Literature, edited by Sandra L. Beckett and Maria Nikolajeva, 49–74. Maryland: Scarecrow Press, 2006.

Neupert, Richard. *French Animation History*. Oxford: John Wiley & Sons, 2011.

Osmond, Andrew. *Spirited Away*. London: British Film Institute, 2008.

"Other Films," *Nausicaa.net* (2010). Available online: http://www.nausicaa.net/wiki/Other_Films

Ōtsuka, Yasuo. *Sakuga Asemamire*. Tokyo: Tokuma Shoten, 2001.

Patten, Fred. *Watching Anime, Reading Manga: 25 Years of Essays and Reviews*. Berkeley: Stone Bridge Press, 2004.

"Prince of the Sun: The Great Adventure of Hols," *Nausicaa.net* (2012). Available online: http://www.nausicaa.net/wiki/Prince_of_the_Sun:The_Great_Adventure_of_Hols

Reinders, Eric. *The Moral Narratives of Hayao Miyazaki*. Jefferson: McFarland & Company, 2016.

Saint-Exupéry, Antoine. *The Little Prince*. London: Bibliophile Books, 1995.

Schodt, Frederik L. *Dreamland Japan: Writings on Modern Manga*. Berkeley: Stone Bridge Press, 1996.

Schodt, Frederik L. *The Astro Boy Essays: Osamu Tezuka and the Manga/Anime Revolution*. Berkeley: Stone Bridge Press, 2007.

Screech, Matthew. "Moebius Nouveau Realism and Science Fiction," in *The Francophone Bande Dessinne*, edited by Charles Forsdick, Laurence Grove, and Libbie McQuillan, 97–114. New York: Rodopi, 2005.

Sharp, Jasper. "Pioneers of Japanese Animation at PIFAN," *Midnight Eye* (2004). Available online: http://www.midnighteye.com/features/pioneers-of-japanese-animation-at-pifan-part–1

Sinibaldi, Caterina. "Dangerous Children and Children in Danger: Reading American Comics under the Italian Fascist Regime," in *The Nation in Children's Literature*, edited by Christopher Kelen and Bjorn Sundmark, 53–69. New York: Routledge, 2013.

Somers, Emily. "An no shinjo [Anne's Feelings]: Politeness and Passion as Anime, Paradox in Takahata's Akage no An," in *Textual Transformations in Children's Literature: Adaptations, Translations, Reconsiderations* edited by Benjamin Lefebvre, 155–174. New York: Routledge, 2015.

Strong, Sarah M. *Miyazawa Kenji's Night of the Milky Way Railway: A Translation and a Guide*. New York: M.E. Sharpe, 1991.

Swale, Alistair. *Anime Aesthetics: Japanese Animation and the "Post-Cinematic" Imagination*. New York: Palgrave Macmillan, 2015.

Takahata, Isao, Miyazaki, Hayao and Kotabe Yōichi. *Maboroshi no Nagagutsu no Pippi*. Tokyo: Iwanami Shobo, 2014.

Tezuka, Osamu. *Astro Boy, Vol. 1*. Milwaukie: Dark Horse Comics, 2002.

Thomas, Daniel. "Miyazaki Comics—The Age of the Flying Boat (1989)." *Ghibli Blog* (2010). Available online: http://ghiblicon.blogspot.co.il/2010/03/miyazaki-comics-age-of-flying-boat–1989.html

Thomas, Daniel. "People of the Desert (Sabaku no Tami)—Hayao Miyazaki's 1969 Manga." *Ghibli Blog* (2014). Available online: http://ghiblicon. blogspot.co.il/2011/04/miyazakis-first-manga-people-of-desert.html

Thomas, Daniel. "Hayao Miyazaki 1972 Pilot Film 'Yuki's Sun.'" *Ghibli Blog* (2015). Available online: http://ghiblicon.blogspot.co.il/2015/02/ hayao-miyazakis-1972-pilot-film-yukis.html

Truffaut, Francois. *The Films in My Life*. New York: Da Capo Press, 1994.

Vandermeer, Jeff and Chambers, S.J. *The Steampunk Bible*. New York: Abrams Image, 2012.

Vera, Noel. "Little Norse Prince (Isao Takahata, 1968)," *A Critic After Dark* (2010). Available online: http://criticafterdark.blogspot.co.il/2010/11/ little-norse-prince-isao-takahata-1968.html

Waley, Arthur. "The Lady who Loved Insects," in *Anthology of Japanese Literature, from the Earliest Era to the Mid-Nineteenth Century*, edited by Donald Keene, New York: Grove Press, 1955.

Williams, Philippe. *The 20th Century, Albert Robida: Translation, Introduction & Critical Material*. Middletown: Wesleyan University Press, 2004.

Wynne Jones, Diana. *Howl's Moving Castle*. New York: HarperCollins, 2001.

Zipes, Jack. *The Enchanted Screen: The Unknown History of Fairy-Tale Films*. New York: Routledge, 2011.

INDEX